Get Up, Stand Up & Rise

THE BEST IS
YET TO COME

Get Up, Stand Up & Rise

THE BEST IS YET TO COME

ELNIEDA TELFER-SINCLAIR

TATE PUBLISHING
AND ENTERPRISES, LLC

Published by Tate Publishing & Enterprises, LLC
127 E. Trade Center Terrace | Mustang, Oklahoma 73064 USA
1.888.361.9473 | www.tatepublishing.com

Tate Publishing is committed to excellence in the publishing industry. The company reflects the philosophy established by the founders, based on Psalm 68:11,
"The Lord gave the word and great was the company of those who published it."

Book design copyright © 2015 by Tate Publishing, LLC. All rights reserved.
Cover design by Ivan Charlem Igot
Interior design by Jomel Pepito

Published in the United States of America

ISBN: 978-1-63306-586-4
1. Biography & Autobiography / Women
2. Biography & Autobiography / Religious
15.02.25

To my children, who have been there
with me through thick and thin;
To my family, who have never known
many of my struggles;
To my friends of over fifty years, who knew
about some of my struggles and have always
told me, "You need to write a book;"
To my friends of over thirty and twenty years, who
have heard my Salvation Messages in seminars
at churches and in the prisons, many of you have
always encouraged me to write a book;
To my friends of ten, five, and less years, who have
never heard my talks or knows very little about me;

Well, friends, here it is,
"Get Up, Stand Up, and Rise: The Best Is Yet to Come!"

Acknowledgments

To the people and ministries used by God to inspire me:

Rev. Billy Graham
Who spoke to me for one week via his television ministry

Bishop Emeritus John Elya
God's holy, loving Santa Claus

Bishop T. D. Jakes
God's powerhouse who says it as it is

Rev. Father David Russell
On fire for the Lord

Rev. Paula White
Her openness and unafraid spirit

Rev. Father Kenneth Ramsay
Calm, full of wisdom

Rev. Father John Bertuluchi
Powerful servant of God

Rev. Father Naim
God's gentle lamb

Mike Murdock
What knowledge

Trinity Broadcasting Network
Inspiration

Matthew Kelley
Who made me do it

Father Pedro (Peter) Puntal
My present priest at St. Vincent de Paul Catholic Church
who is so practical and present to our everyday living

My numerous friends
Some in and some out of the family of God

Inga Hartnett
My best friend for over 40 years

My prayer angels
Always there in time of prayer

Once again, to my children
Who were my blessings in disguise. Why? Because of them,
giving up was not an option. I was forced *to push on*

———— ❦ ————

With all my heart, I would like to thank
Tate Publishing for taking my manuscript
and transforming it into this book.
You knew this was my first attempt at writing
a book, so you skillfully led me through
each step with your wonderful staff.
My special thanks to the project manager assigned to
me, the editor, the photography department, everyone.
Please know that I could not have done
it without you. Thanks so much.
May God richly bless you all.

Contents

As you read this book, please feel free to make it yours by changing the *my's* to *ours* in the titles because I know we all go through these Seasons, Storms, and Victories. I want to relate to each of you, to laugh and cry with you, as one person to another—yet leave you with hope for each day knowing that if *I* can continue, then *so can you.*

Introduction

This book is written from the heart of a Jamaican woman who was so hurt by the mistakes she made in life.

She wants to let other hurting people know that there is a *way* out.

Do you feel as if you are in a box with
four tight walls and no way out?
Did you put yourself in this box?
Did someone throw you in this box?
Did circumstances drop you in this box?
Whatever the reason,
my brothers and sisters, you *can* get out!
Just look up, look up to your Creator who created you.
Wonderfully and fearfully He created you.
Since He formed you, He can re-create
you, change you, and
give you the courage to
"get up, stand up, and rise!"

My First Life

The Villages, Florida 32163

First life? Some may ask. Is there a first and second life here on earth? I thought she was alive? She is alive, isn't she? Or, is she dead?

From Childhood/Teenage

I was born on the island of Jamaica, in the West Indies, to parents who worked hard for their three children. We were far from wealthy, yet we lacked nothing. Life was full of fun and happy times. At the same time, we were deadly afraid of our mother. We didn't know why, but even if we thought of something bad, somehow she would know it. We would whisper to ourselves, "What's with her? How can she know even our thoughts?" We dared not lie to her because she would find out, and all hell would break loose. She was known in the area as the Crazy Jew, so we were able to go anywhere we pleased as no one dared mess with us. Don't get me wrong, SHE LOVED US, would do any and everything for us. But she protected us like a lioness.

To Teenage/Young Woman

I was married at the age of eighteen without my parents' consent. My father, the best father in the world, was a sailor; his ship traveled the world. We always looked forward to the times he would come home because it would be happy party times. Everyone was elated when he came home.

Because Papa was always at sea, Mama was the ruler of the house—and rule she did. Mama was a very strong half-Jewish woman, with her father from Israel, and her mother from Brazil.

Mama was strongly against my friendship with my then boyfriend. One day he came to visit me. While I was standing beside his car talking with him, Mama got so angry, she ran inside the house, got all my clothes, and threw them on the sidewalk. Frantic that she would kill me, I jumped into his car and we drove off. This *made* us decide to marry even though I was only eighteen and he was twenty.

> Young people, please, please, listen to your parents. They know so much more than you, even though they may not be able to articulate what they are trying to tell you. BUT believe me, they know from their experiences.

To Marriage

Innocent as we were about the facts of life, we had three children, each one a year apart. Early into the marriage, I realized that beneath my husband's handsome face was a bad temper. This temper changed his personality and actually made him not only cruel, but ugly in my sight. He would beat me even when I was eight months pregnant. Once, he sliced me with a knife on my arm. I still have that scar. He ran after me with a cutlass, drew a gun at me, broke a plate with food over my head, etc. It took me all night to wash and comb that food and grease out of my hair. There were times I went to work with a black eye, suffering the humiliation of people staring at me.

After each beating, I would leave him. I left him fifteen times. Even though my mother had insisted that I should not marry him, she did not attend the wedding, nor did she allow my younger sister to attend; naturally, after these beatings, having nowhere else to go, I would run back to my mother. That was my only home.

The last time I left him, I was pregnant but I did not know it. We both knew I had missed my period, but we thought nothing of it. Now, however, because we were separated, when I discovered I was pregnant, it became *news* around town. This pregnancy news went fast. As soon as it reached his ears, he told everyone it was not his child, that's why I had left him. His true friends knew better, they became angry with him, especially a promising young boxer friend he had.

My ex knew that I was always an innocent young woman; he knew he was the first man for me; he knew I knew nothing from nothing, only what he had taught me; he knew he was always bragging to his friends about how he took my virginity.

He had a surprise coming though, because when this child was born, he went secretly to the hospital to see the baby, without telling anyone. That day I opened my eyes and saw him crying over me.

He said, "I am sorry, please forgive me. I told everyone it was not my child, but as I entered the room, the nurse said to me, Come this way your baby is over here.'"

He said, he asked, "How do you know I have a baby here?"
She replied, "The baby looks just like you."

He said, "When I saw the baby, I almost passed out because this baby is our only child that has my distinct resemblance."

As fate would have it, because he told these silly lies about the baby, this child had more of him than our first two children. Incidentally, he would always kneel and cry at my feet after beating me, saying he was sorry, etc. I never knew what it was all about until I became a grown woman living in the States and heard that it was domestic abuse.

After five years of hell with him, leaving him fifteen times, then going back to my mother, only to be cursed by her with, "I told you so, etc. etc." I had to run from her again, and with nowhere else to go—you guessed it—back to him, my life became a nightmare.

This back and forth went on and on, until one night while living at my mother's house, a young man who was boarding with her at that time, sat down and had a talk with me. He said, "You have to stop this running. I feel so sorry for you. You are suffering so much. You must stand up for yourself and make a decision to stay in one place, choose to stay with your husband or your mother but you must do something." Not wanting to burden my mother, I decided to return to my husband and let him face the responsibilities of taking care of his children.

Soon after however, his cruelty started all over again. Finally, one day I could take his beating no longer, so I waited until he left for work, swallowed my pride, packed the children in a taxi, taking nothing except the clothes on my back, clothing and formulas for the children, and went back to my mother.

The taxi drove up; my mother was sitting on the verandah. As soon as she saw us, the babies were one, two, and three years old, she stood up. I thought to myself, *Here we go again, she is going to start screaming and cursing bloody hell, but* this time, *I was ready for it.*

To my surprise, mama *came outside to meet us. Without a word, she was reaching for the children, taking their stuff and helping me out of the car as calm as can be.* I was amazed, *this time* she actually welcomed us in her home. I could not believe it! It was so ironic because *this time* I had vowed to myself, "I don't care how she curses me, what she says or does to me, *this time,* I am staying—whatever—it will be better than the hell I am in. I will get a job, I will clean floors if I have to, but my children and I will *never, ever starve."* (Please hold that "clean floor" thought—there is an old Jamaican saying that goes, "Be careful what you say because what comes out of your mouth will come back to bite you later." More about this "clean floor" in my New York Experiences.)

After the taxi left and we were all inside, Mama told me that Granny, my deceased grandmother, had come to her in a dream last night and told her that—"Your daughter would be coming home and that *this time* you should not get angry with her, but welcome her instead."

The words *this time* never meant anything to me, until I started writing this book. Now that I am so much older and wiser, I can truly say, I understand.

I understand how disappointed my mother was in me. The mere fact that I disobeyed her when I was a beautiful young girl, with my whole life ahead of me, messing it up with a bad marriage then coming back to her with three babies! No wonder she lost it with me. I would have gone bananas.

Starting Life Again—this Time, Alone with My Children

To the Workforce

Within three days, I began working as a legal secretary with a law firm. Where did I get the clothes to go to work? My younger sister allowed me to wear her clothes. *It was agreed* that I would wake up at 5:00 a.m. every day, handwash all the babies' clothes five dozen diapers, their sheets and bedding in order to hang them out to dry before the tenants got up (after my eldest sister left for London to study and I got married, leaving only my youngest sister at home, my mother had rented out half of the house) before I left for work then when they were dried, my sister would put them away, and bathe and feed my children. Mama would prepare the meals. When I got paid, I would give my sister a little compensation. When I got home, I would take over my children. We had a plan and we worked that plan.

Eventually I spoke with the attorneys I was working with about my predicament. The firm decided to handle my divorce case for a minimal fee.

Fifteen Cases of Cruelty

I was represented by a then young, promising, and vibrant attorney (now deceased). The day of the hearing, he and I stood in the front of the court as the judge started reading out the cases one by one. This was my first time in any courtroom, and I was dazed but at the same time fascinated by the process of the system. As he read them, tears started rolling down my face, but I stood as still as a piece of wood. When the judge reached the fifth case he said, "This divorce will be granted, unless contested." At the time, I had no idea that my husband,was in the back of the courtroom. So when he heard what the judge had said, he responded, "I have no idea where she got fifteen cases of cruelty because I only hit her once or twice."

When I heard his voice, I was too afraid to turn around and look at him, but knowing him and his arrogance, I could have imagined his attitude because the judge looked at him, took off his glasses, placed them down, and said to him, "Would you like me to continue reading the cases?"

I then said, "Your Honor, it is actually sixteen cases because just last week my sister, our helper, and I took the children to the King's Theatre to see a movie; apparently, he was there because as soon as the movie ended, he jumped over all the seats trying to get to me with his fists. All of us started screaming, and the theatre called the police. When the police arrived, he told the police that I took his children away from him and my "stinking mother" wouldn't let him come to see them. The police told him not to go near me, and they took us home."

While I was talking to the judge, I had no idea what my husband was doing, but knowing him, I knew it was not good, because all of a sudden the judge shouted, looking straight at him and said, "Stand still, you are in the Queen's Court, not in the King's Theatre. I can imagine why her mother doesn't want you near her daughter, and should not allow you near her, unless you decide to visit as you did when you were courting her. You married her daughter and beat her fifteen times?" The judge continued, "This divorce will be granted not based on these fifteen outlined cases of cruelty, but merely on the first three cases." With this, he turned to me and said, "and, if he ever comes near you again without your permission, if he ever lays another finger on you, I want you to let me know personally, *and* we will deal with him." My mind was in such turmoil, I did not know whether to laugh or cry. I just kept shaking my head in a yes gesture while thinking of the nearest exit from that place. I wanted to run for my life before he caught up with me outside. I watched him dashing for the parking lot, and so I ran in the opposite direction. I ran through the back streets, all one-way streets to avoid him, to my office which was not too far from the courthouse. I ran up the stairs. I peeked through the window and saw him drive up and down the street looking for me, but he was too late. I was safe inside.

By the way, my sister had gone to court with me as my witness, but she was never called so he did not see her. I did not even think about her in my haste to run for my life. My sister was my only witness. I did not ask anyone else because I did not want him to know I was divorcing him. She and I had talked about it, and we decided not to say a word to Mama. I made this decision because Mama was so angry over this marriage and its ordeal she would always say, "I did not make any marriage and I am not breaking any marriage, she put herself into it, let her take herself out of it." Mama wanted nothing to do with it at all. She was only concerned about her three grandchildren. She loved them dearly and would attack and kill even a fly if that fly had the nerve to land on them.

Little did we know, two days later, not only our mother would know, but that all of Jamaica would. We had no idea that someone from one of Jamaica's Newspaper, *The Star*, was present in the courtroom, and that they would print the entire divorce drama in the center spread of their paper. The heading was: "When a Wife Was Five Months Pregnant, Her Husband Said to Her, Guess What? Another Woman Is Pregnant for Me Again: An Argument Ensued Followed by His Beating Her." They printed everything that went on in the courtroom.

I knew nothing about this article, I went home from work that evening as usual, only to find my mother and all the tenants in the backyard laughing and dancing with the paper in their hands. As soon as my mother saw me, she shouted, "You did it, you did it, Thank God, you did it." I looked at my sister thinking, *what happened, what did I do?* my mother then flashed the paper before me. I took it and read it. I could not believe my eyes. My sister and I had planned to wait until the divorce papers came from the court, then surprise her with it, but the newspapers beat us to it.

I had another battle. My husband refused to give me money for the children because he said that I would not be able to make it on my own with three babies; therefore, when we were hungry, I would come back to him. He also said that with three children I would be a burden to men; therefore, no man would ever want me. Innocent as I was, I believed him. Because those words were imprinted on my mind, I vowed that I would die of starvation before going back to him. I also vowed that no other man would ever use or take advantage of me. I *hated* men.

For over seven years after the divorce, I kept away from men. With this hatred and those words in my mind, I jumped wholeheartedly with my eyes wide open and my feet solidly placed on the ground; I ventured into *my world*; I became a bitch on wheels.

To My World

For years I worked at various law firms in Jamaica. Dating men here and there. Eventually, I decided to leave Jamaica because I knew, financially, I could not make it on the island. I left Jamaica, leaving the children with my mother, and moved to New York City. For a young woman in her twenties, leaving a small island and landing in New York there by herself was a SHOCK in itself. My experiences there will be in Seasons of my Life.

To New York, New York—Starting Life Over Again

Living in New York made me realize that no job was degrading. A job was a job. Like it or not. It took a while to develop that attitude, but I remember writing to my mother (God bless her soul) in tears about jobs I had to do. She replied, "Never you cry over any honest job you do because whatever you have in your head, no man can take it out." To this day, I cannot understand how my mother, with the limited education she had, knew those words to say to me. That was the turning point in my life. Talk about...

My Return to Jamaica and Starting Life Over Again

After three years in New York, working and saving, I returned to Jamaica, stronger and so much wiser. While living in New York, I realized *that* I was young and beautiful. Never knew or even thought about that before—ever wonder why Shakespeare said, "Youth is wasted on the young?"—that's one portion of it. I realized *that* my ex-husband was wrong. Men wanted me, even with three children.

Because of my job experiences in New York, I had no qualms in taking any job when I returned to Jamaica. Even though I studied court reporting in New York, I decided to go back to secretarial work because it was paying more than the court reporting. I began working the next week after returning to Jamaica as a secretary in various firms, various because if any firm offered me more salary than I was receiving, I was gone. I needed the extra funds.

Purchasing My First Home

One day I saw a full page article in the newspapers advertising a new housing development named Independent City. I had no idea where it was located, but that did not bother me. My interest was the mortgage payment of $64.00 per month for a three-bedroom, two-bathroom house. I figured, if I am now paying rent of $68.00, why not pay it for a mortgage? I needed the deposit fast.

I went to the bank, without any funds, spoke with the bank manager, who was a distant friend, to ask for the deposit. He wanted to know how I would be able to pay both the mortgage and the loan at the same time. I pointed out to him that I was presently paying rent of $68.00 and that the mortgage would be $64.00, so I could afford it. I also told him that after leaving the bank, I was heading to the Sheraton Hotel to be interviewed for a night hostess position. The salary from this night job would be deposited directly into the bank to repay this loan.

It took hours trying to convince him, but just as I thought he was going to say no, he said, "Listen, I know you mean well and you are a fighter, but my job is on the line here, I am going to lend you the deposit, but you must promise that you will not let me down, my job is at stake."

I promised, got the loan, ran all the way to the sales office, made the deposit, (still having no idea where the house was), drove up town to The Sheraton for the interview, was about to leave because the line of applicants was through the door, when the head of a man popped through the door, looked down the line, I had popped my head out as soon as the door opened, our eyes met, he yelled to me, "Are you the person who I just spoke with on the phone"? I quickly caught on and said yes. He said, "Come in, you are the last person we will see today."

"Mama Mia!" I said, "Thank you, Lord"—and ran in. Once inside, he said, "I am so glad you answered because there was no phone call, I spoke with no one; I just wanted to get rid of the crowd because I was not going to hire any of them." He continued, "This is not a chambermaid job, this is a hostess job, I have no idea what they think they were applying for." I smiled and thought to myself, *If only you knew, if only you knew I once worked as a chambermaid in New York.* What a world, we all have our prejudices. I got the job!

I worked as a secretary from 8:00 a.m. to 4:00 p.m., then as a hostess from 5:00 p.m. to 2:00 a.m. On the first evening of my night job, I went home with swollen feet from the high heels. I knew then exactly what the Beatles meant when they sang, "A Hard Days Night." Funny how words we usually throw in the air can land on us later with meanings. As the years went by, I also had to work weekends and holidays, floating with agencies. I never took vacations. I worked with the agencies during my vacation periods, so I could have double salaries.

I vividly remember one Christmas morning, I had to work with an insurance company on Harbour Street. I was the only person walking on the street that day, one of the busiest streets in Kingston. I cried all the way to the job. I had left the house early, so I could be back in time to fix Christmas dinner and take the children to a movie.

Working in the hotel industry as a hostess was like a nightly holiday for me.

It broke my monotonous secretarial day stress, giving me a chance to enjoy music, people, dancing, and fun, even if I could not take a vacation. That was my vacation, until I started meeting men from all over the world. I met men who would take me to places I had only read about, local and international men, professional men—men of stature, men in high places, wealthy, classy, polished men. My lifestyle changed, I refused to go out with just any men, especially men who, in the back of my mind, were similar to my ex. Men who would beat you, then turn around and want to go to bed with you. Men who could never afford to give you a dime, never knew how to treat a woman, then turned around and discussed the women they dated with their male friends. Please!

Because I dated a different quality of men, my hatred of men subsided. However, I still kept them at a distance. I would never trust them all the way. I made a vow that no man would ever use me again. My thoughts were, *they want to get into my pants, I will get into their pockets.* My motto: Tit for Tat.

I began studying men. I asked them questions. I would sit and talk with them for hours. I enjoyed talking and talking with them. Needless to say, I learned a lot from them. In my zeal of wanting to know, I discovered that decent, educated, intelligent men, whether they were local or international, had more or less the same desires. Some were unfaithful, but they loved their wives and children. Some just wanted a nice woman to dine and have fun with in different places, often a place far from home, etc. But one thing I did learn was that they were completely the opposite of some of the dumb-ass men I met in my earlier years. My mother was right: "You are young, you have the world before you."

Working as a secretary on Duke Street (at that time the "Park Avenue" of Jamaica), there were certain elite places you could go for lunch. I knew the Duke Street secretaries were tearing me to pieces, pointing at me behind my back and whispering, "She is working as an hostess at nights at the Sheraton." Demeaning in their eyes, but what they did not know was:

> That I had three children to support;
> That I would never beg;
> That we would never go hungry;
> That I would never, ever go back to my husband;
> That I just returned from New York, where I worked at any job I got;
> That in New York, I had determined in my mind, that if a beautiful woman like me could grab a mop and pail and work as a chambermaid (among other jobs, demeaning in their eyes), then I could and

would use that same beauty to work, as a cocktail hostess, and, may I add, in one of the finest hotels in Jamaica;

That I would always remember what my mother had told me, "Any honest job."

What they did not know was

That I had the last laugh on them, because I would watch them stroll into the lounge for happy hour after work, with their nose in the air, holding on the arms of Tom or John, thinking they were such a hit, but...

What they truly did not know was

That they were just the third or fourth girl he had brought in for the evening while they thought they were "the only one."

It was amusing for us hostesses to wait and see who was coming and going with whom. They would even be more shocked to know that those same men sat together and discussed the evenings they had with them. What a laugh we had. THAT'S one of the main reasons I dated foreigners—they would be gone the next day. I would have lunch money for my children, food on the table, salary for the maid, shoes for our feet, mortgage payment, etc.

No more borrowing from friends and neighbors "until payday." I had it! If you had money, Honey, I'd love you. No money, Honey, keep walking, I don't love you!!

You'd say...Wrong idea, Elnieda! Yes, of course, but I knew no better then. All I thought about was survival for myself and my children. After all, this was *my first life, remember?* At that time, wrong or right, I refused to let any man sleep with me all night, get up and leave, then I would have to turn around and borrow lunch money from my neighbors for my children to go to school. I thought, *Something is wrong with this picture*, so I ceased dating the average man. I dated men who would take me places I could not afford to go. Ambassadors, overseas pilots, owners of major overseas corporations setting up businesses in Jamaica, dignitaries, etc. These men would not ask if you had a need, they were intelligent enough to know you *had* a need, and they gave, gave without your asking. God bless each one of them.

With all this, I thought I was safe. Never gave a thought about the unseen eyes who were watching my every move—but remember, I was in *my world*.

Finally, I met a wonderful Jamaican man. He was eight years younger than I. He moved in with me and the children. I was able to quit my night job. After years of living together, I knew our relationship was going nowhere. Not because of the age difference but because I knew he would one day want children of his own. I wanted no more children. His parents were devoted Christians. I was not. They would never accept me with three children for their son. Not to mention, I was always fighting off women from him, so we called it quits. We have remained friends to this day. A wonderful, exceptional man.

My Dream Home

At age thirty-nine, I was able to purchase my dream three-storey house in New Kingston. I was then working as accounts executive in a large downtown hotel at that time and decided life was good. I was not rich but I had enough. I decided I would semi-retire. I planned on working three days per week at the hotel. *Please note the I's in this paragraph.* All this time, I had no idea there was a master planner who had the final say. Remember the rich fool with his vineyards who wanted to build larger barns to store all his excessive treasures? Funny, how you dream of having something—then you get it—but it never serves the purpose you intended it for. The idea of my dream house was that my children would live in a little luxury, but by the time this was accomplished, my two older children were already living in the USA, which I will expound on in the chapter, "Seasons of My Life," my youngest was the only child living with me in this three-story, four-bedroom, three-bath townhouse.

To Socialism

Jamaica was embracing socialism. I did not know the pros and cons of this because I was not tuned in with politics, so I figured this would not affect me; I am just an ordinary middle-class working woman. As time went on, I realized that the Masses of the people *were* the ones who did not know what socialism meant. I found out, by their conversations, that they thought it meant they could pack up their belongings and move into any house, any home, with any family they chose or wanted to, and share, and share alike. I had a huge, boarded front gate. One day the "street cleaners" were on the outer side cleaning, and I was on the inner side sitting when one of them said, "Next day after socialism, this is the house me moving into." They were talking about my house. I just smiled because I had my gate as protection.

Crime was at its peak, yet I was not alarmed because I told myself it was political, and since I am not involved in politics (although in previous years, I was secretary to the mayor of Kingston), I am safe.

A couple of days later, my girlfriend who lived next door called out to me and said that, "Last night they shot and killed the Oriental girl behind her gate." She lived two doors away from us. We were all in shock. The following week, the husband of a close friend of mine and one of his coworkers were shot as he left work. They both worked on Harbour Street. While other co-workers were driving him to the hospital, they said he kept pleading with them, saying over and over, "Please don't let me die, please don't let me die." They took him to the public hospital, but the place was overcrowded, so they drove him to a private hospital. On arrival, he was dead. This was it for me. I needed no more convincing. I said, "I am out of here."

My daughter, who was then living in California, had to return to Jamaica for her reentry into the States. I planned to leave with her. My youngest son insisted on staying in Jamaica because of school. He said he could take care of himself and the house. I rented out the second floor to the Food and Beverage manager at the hotel. He would give my son a helping hand.

With the IMF and then Austerity, there was no foreign currency in the banks. Jamaicans leaving were allowed to take out a maximum of US$50.00. Only problem was, by the time I decided to leave, the banks did not have the US$50.00. A friend who lived two doors from me, loaned me US$12.00. That was the amount of money I had when I left Jamaica and landed at Miami International Airport.

At age 28, Formal night as hostess,
Sheraton Hotel, Kingston, Jamaica

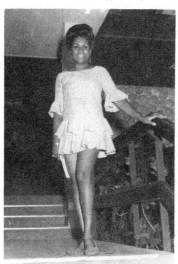

At age 28, Casual night as hostess, Sheraton
Hotel, Kingston, Jamaica

My Second Life

The Villages, Florida 32163

Miami here I come, starting life again

I arrived in Miami, Wednesday night, October 11, 1978, with my daughter, who had returned to Jamaica for her appointment with me at the American Embassy and her re-entry into the States. We landed at MIA with the US$12.00 in my pocket that I had borrowed from my friend in Jamaica. The taxi charged us $15 to go where we were staying. A "friend" who was already in Miami had found a room for us in the home of a Jamaican woman. She had a sort of rooming house. Luckily, she was Jamaican, so she understood the plight of Jamaicans arriving. She had to lend me $5.00 ($2.00 tip) to pay the balance the taxi charged us, leaving me flat broke.

Here we were at this woman's home with no money to pay her. She said the room was $50 per week; I explained to her that as soon as I got a job, I would pay her. Bless her heart, she understood, she gave us tea in the morning, loaned us quarters for bus fare, and gave us directions to the express bus stop. We went downtown to look for jobs. I went to Florida National Bank, Thursday, and the following day, Friday, they called and offered me a job. I started work the next Monday.

My daughter kept telling me how great California was compared to Miami. She wanted us to go to California. She insisted that if I went to California, I would love it and would prefer to stay there. I had nothing to lose really because I was exploring, so the first paycheck I got, I used it to pay the landlady and purchase two one-way tickets to California.

My ex-brother-in-law and my eldest son met us at the airport. One of the main reasons why I decided to go to California was to see my son again; it was worth it. For the couple of years I did not see him, he had sprung up in height way over my head into a handsome teenager.

The doctor my daughter was working with in California, before she left for re-entry, sent me to a doctor friend of hers at a clinic the following Monday for an interview. They hired me. We stayed for a couple of days with my brother-in-law, who helped us find a two-bedroom apartment. Of course we had no furniture, so we had to sleep on the floor for a couple of days. By this time, my son, who was also staying with my brother-in-law, going to school during the days and working at nights, moved in with us. We figured with the three of us working, we could make it.

After a few days, we purchased two beds from the Salvation Army and a table with four chairs. I decided, hell, I was going to call my ex-husband, who had his own business in California, and tell him we needed help. After all, he owed me years of support for the children. Surprisingly, he was very nice on the phone and that evening he took us to dinner, we talked and he promised to pick me up that Saturday morning to purchase some furniture for us. The kids did not believe it, but he kept his word. He purchased a living room set for us and took us grocery shopping. My daughter got a job at May's Department Store. We had a start and were on our way.

One thing I did not bargain for, or know about, was the earthquakes. It turned me off from California and I wanted to return to Miami. Secondly, my daughter wanted to do her own thing, live her own life, so as the old saying goes, "Two bulls cannot rule in one pen," I decided, "Let me out of here." I figured they both had a place to live, beds to sleep on, etc., so they could work and pay the rent between themselves. I headed back to Miami.

No sooner had I arrived in Miami than my youngest son, who insisted that he wanted to stay in Jamaica, started calling every day, collect of course, saying that he wanted to come to America. Of course I did not have the airfare to Jamaica. I had moved back into the rooming house. One day the landlady heard our telephone conversations. It so happened that she had some things she wanted to send to Jamaica, so she bought the ticket for me with the understanding that I would take the things to Jamaica for her and repay her for the ticket later. This worked out well for me.

I went to Jamaica, took my son to the embassy, got his entry papers, gave notice to the tenants living in the house, and shipped my furniture and belongings to Miami. I figured, while they were en route, I would find an apartment.

Five days after returning to Miami with my son, he decided that he wanted to go to California to his father. I think he missed his brother and sister. His father sent him a ticket and he left. I thought, maybe it was best also because I knew he would not have been able to live at this rooming house and be comfortable because he was spoilt. This would take a long time explaining. My other children insisted that I spoilt him because he was the baby. Which to me was not true!

In a few days I got a better job on Brickell Avenue, closer to home. Hence, I discovered Brickell Avenue; it was plush. I liked it and felt more relaxed. I saved enough for an apartment. The landlady told me about some apartments close by. Sure enough, I went and got an apartment there. It was so convenient. The express bus ran directly from there to my office on Brickell in the heart of Downtown Miami. I moved in and, again, slept on the floor for three months, until my furniture arrived. Sleeping on the floor for three months is easy to write on paper, but it was horrible. It was in this apartment that my life took a hundred-eighty-degree right-about turn. Nothing that I had anticipated, nothing that I was looking for, nothing that I gave second thoughts to, or nothing that I could ever have dreamt or imagined.

Remember I was coming to Miami to pick up my life once more after losing again and again, this time to politics. Remember I had the future all worked out. I would just go back to working two jobs. I would meet more men to help me. But something else was in store for me.

To Being Born-again

I lived on the seventh floor. I woke up one dark, rainy Saturday with my body racking in pain from sleeping on the hard floor so many months that I started to cry. My crying turned to screaming and my screaming turned into cursing at God (please don't ask me why the minute something/anything bad happens to us, the first person we blame is God, because I don't know). All I know is that I was cursing and screaming at God, for over 15 minutes, yelling, "Why did You let this happen to me? I worked hard all my life. I never hurt anyone. I have suffered and suffered trying to make it. I had to leave my big four-bedroom, three-story house in Jamaica, to come here and live in a one bedroom apartment, sleeping on the floor, my body is hurting, my neck is hurting, I feel like nothing, I don't want to live like this, I can't live like this!" (As if sitting on the floor and cursing at *him* was not enough, or perhaps I thought *he* was not hearing me, I got up, walked over to the window, I could hardly see with the tears in my eyes, so I pointed my finger to the sky and screamed, "Hey, Jesus, I know you are out there somewhere because I read about you in Sunday School, so I know you are there, and if you are real, YOU BETTER SHOW ME YOU!"

I know now, but I did not know then, that the minute you question the legitimate realness of God, *he* shows up. I know now because later on in my walk with God, I have heard testimonies (had no clue what a testimony was at the time), upon testimonies with this same question, "IF YOU ARE REAL." Now, every time I hear those words, it brings a smile to my face, knowing what will follow. He shows up!

As I said before, it was a dark rainy Saturday afternoon, not a streak of sun in the sky. I had barely ended my ranting, raging, and cursing, quietly sobbing and calming down, when I suddenly heard the whirl of a strong wind. It picked up with intensity, like a sort of whirlwind, something like a hurricane force; through my tears, I tried opening my eyes to see what was happening. I looked down through the window, nothing was moving, the trees were not moving, yet I could see and hear this whirling force moving through the clouds like a twirling ball. It was coming closer and closer towards me. Then a swaying, strange feeling came over me, and I thought to myself, *It must be an earthquake.* I kept staring. All of a sudden, it became like a huge ball of fire in the sky; it was coming straight at me. Then I thought this is the end of the world with fire and brimstone but the more I stared the more I realized that the rest of the place below me, was as calm as could be. I shouted, "What the hell?" And then, only then did I realize what was happening. I shouted loudly, "Oh, my God, God is real, you idiot, you cursed God, and now he is going to kill you, oh my God, oh my God!" I screamed. I felt as if I was going to faint, so I tried to grab and hold the window sill, but it was made of marble, and my nails were too long, so I kept losing my grip. Still staring at the ball of fire coming towards me, but too paralyzed to move, I watched it coming straight at me through the glass window. It hit me slam bang in the face. I fell back on the floor as if someone had pushed me down. I landed on my back.

While I was falling, my eyes caught a glimpse of a clock radio, lying on a small towel I had on the floor, which was my bedside table, the time was three o'clock something. I passed out. Later, when I opened my eyes I felt strange. I was as light as a feather; the apartment was so quiet, it was as if time had stood still. I looked at the clock, it said six o'clock something. I thought to myself, *You slept for three hours? What happened?* I looked around because it felt as if someone was in the apartment with me, then I remembered the incident. I wanted to run but I could not get up, so I shuffled backwards on my hands and buttocks pushing myself towards the door. I got up and ran downstairs to my neighbors on the second floor.

As soon as they saw me, they asked, "What happened to you? You look as if you saw a ghost."

I said to myself, *Keep your mouth shut, if you tell anyone that you cursed God, He came into your apartment and knocked you out, they are going to put you in a straight jacket,* so I said, "Nothing, nothing happened."

Normally when I visited these friends, I would stay a few minutes, perhaps now and then fifteen minutes. This day however, I stayed and stayed until I could see they wanted to retire for the night, so I left.

I walked into my apartment, but I was no longer afraid. I knew a quiet presence was there. It was so peaceful, I just sat on the floor with my back against the wall. I thought to myself, *You need to read the Bible.* I knew I had a small New Testament somewhere so I told myself I would look for it tomorrow. I had no idea what had happened to me but I knew I had a sudden urge to read the Bible.

I flipped on the television. This was an old TV I had bought for $25.00. It only had one working channel. Billy Graham was on. Normally, if I turned on the radio or TV, and there were Christian programs, I would keep going until I found something else. This night, I was so exhausted, tired, and dazed I just wanted to be still and see something, anything. With one station, I had no choice so I gazed at it. Since this was the first time I was seeing this sort of program, I had no idea that Billy Graham, at the end of his sermons, usually points his finger at the camera and says, "Now don't forget, go to church on Sunday." You have to realize how bummed out I was because I thought he was talking to me and me alone, I was so out of tune, I didn't think that millions of people were watching him. I remember saying to myself, "Go to church? I have not gone to Church in over twenty years, the roof would cave in if I walked into a church."

I was born-again but had no clue, since I knew nothing about this sort of thing and knew nothing about what had happened to me.

The next day, I found the New Testament, but I was in for more surprises and more of Billy Graham than I had bargained for, because he was on again, Sunday night, and Monday night and...you guessed it—he was having a crusade, Hello!

This was the beginning of my thirty-four years walking with the Lord. As time passed, I truly began growing with him in leaps and bounds.

One day, shortly after my born-again experience. I sat down and started to think about my life. I wondered what in heaven's name it was all about. Here I was living in America, after all the years of working, toiling, slaving, sinning to get the things I wanted—here I was with nothing. I was living in a one-bedroom apartment. I really had a hard long look at myself and my life. I said to myself, "What have I really accomplished or achieved in all my life"

The last house I purchased was my heart's desire. I really was planning on living it up. I had enough to retire in 1978, could afford to work only two or three days per week, now this?

God must have been laughing all along or maybe just pitying me because I did not live in this dream house for more than a year. As a matter of fact, two of my children were in the States before the purchase of this house, and one of them never lived in it at all. Yet, the main reason why I had gone overboard to buy this house in New Kingston was that each child could have their own bedroom since the first house had three bedrooms. This had four bedrooms. I sat and I thought, *What was it all about?* I lost it all in one year, and here I was with nothing.

I started to pray and cry out to the Lord, "Father God, wherever my children are, touch them and let them know you are there with them, forgive my ex-husband for straying from these children, forgive me for marrying him without my parents' consent, forgive me for having three children with him, wash me, wash me, forgive me, forgive me." I remember when that was not enough, I laid down on my stomach, continued praying and crying until I was so weak, I fell asleep on the floor. I had also promised God that if he did the things I asked, from this day on I would obey him and do all the things he wanted me to do.

When I awoke, I felt that same light-feathery feeling as the day I was born-again. Later in my walk, I learned that it was the "cleansing feeling." I was frightened and yet happy. I was afraid also because I had heard people say that when you make a promise to God don't break it. At the time I was making these promises, I was carried away going on and on not understanding most of what I was saying, but I trusted God and knew that he knew. Eventually, my youngest son returned to Miami, but we always had head butting arguments.

Through it all, I knew that he was always a God-fearing child. I know he would go to the church services held at the Sheraton Hotel on Saturday mornings when I was asleep. I felt I did not have to go to church because God was in my heart. My son, however, insisted that I did not know God. He insisted that if I knew God, I would not be going to nightclub after nightclub, I would not be cursing four-letter words, I would not be going around with homosexuals and having them as my friends, I would not have intimate men friends. I would yell back at him, "I know God because I am a Christian and because I believe that Jesus is the Son of God."

Satan was really fooling me into believing that I was all right because I honestly thought that knowing that Jesus was God was it. Really? Now I know differently. Now I know *that* the devil also knows that Jesus is the Son of God, but he is not saved. Now I know *that*, "Not only those who say 'Lord' will enter the kingdom of heaven, but those who know the will of my Father and do it, will be saved. Amen. (Matt 7:21)." Now I know so much more.

Looking back on my life, sometimes I cry, sometimes I feel ashamed, and sometimes I just shudder. I can't imagine how I could have been so stupidly blind. I had no idea that you have to admit your sins, confess them to God, repent, ask him to make you whole, so he can dwell within you. Be baptized, and then you would be born-again.

Born-again? What's that? How dare anyone try to tell me about being born-again, especially my children. Whenever they went to this Pastor Wright Crusade in the park in Jamaica, I would laugh at them and call him Pastor Wrong. When they started confronting me about God, I would send them flying with four-letter words. I would tell them that the stupid church they were attending was worshipping fallen angels and that was the reason they were speaking in tongues.

Baptism? What's that? How dare they to tell me that I have to be baptized to enter the kingdom of heaven. I would send them flying again. I would let them know that I was baptized as a baby by the Father in the Catholic Church, and I did not need any more baptism.

After all this, I had the nerve to wonder why my life was upside down.

Brothers and sisters, when we have no one to turn to but God, he will open our eyes, so we can see the wrong things we are doing and have done. Things that we did, not even realizing they were wrong, we were so blind. We were so lost, wandering down the wrong path and not even knowing it. I tell you, God loves us so much that when he says it is time for us to come home, he means it is time. Then and only then, can we look up and truly sing about his "Amazing Grace." Then and only then can we truly sing "He placed my feet on solid ground," or "On Christ, the solid rock I stand." All these songs would come alive to us. His word comes alive to us. *All things become new to us.*

Thank God that although I left him, he never left me. If he had given up on me, I don't know where I would have been today. But God was ready for me, I was so cornered, I had to say, "Oh God, help me, show me, change me. I am sorry for all I have done. Reach out, reach out to my children wherever they are today and touch them." And on and on I went, that was my confessing part of it. God then says, "If you acknowledge me before men, I will acknowledge you before my Father who is in heaven, if you deny me, I will deny you." After my confession and repentance at home, I felt the urge to go to church, so I started praying, asking God to find a church for me. One morning, God sent Dee Dee, an angel, to lead me into a church .

Dee Dee came into my life

Hi Elnieda:

I really enjoyed reading the portion of your book. You're an inspiration to me and I know will be to many, many people. I thank God often for allowing me to meet you on the bus that day. No only did I gain a wonderful friend, coworker, even sister, but I also can look at all you have done for the Lord's Kingdom over the years and think how blessed I am to know you. You have done great things for Christ and have ministered to uncounted numbers of people in more than one nation. I haven't done any of that, but I often think the most important thing I have ever done in my life was to invite you to come to church with me.

I am humbled and amazed at what a wonderful servant of God you are, and I hope God will remember my small part in your returning to Him all those years ago in South Miami

Sincerely,
Dee Dee Stewart
First Baptist Church of South Miami

The only time I could find to read my Bible was riding the bus in the mornings to work. This particular morning, I was seated, reading the little New Testament I had found, when all of a sudden I heard, "Praise the Lord, you are a Christian!" I was shocked. I could not believe anyone could be so bold as to say that out loud, *on the bus*! I looked up at her. She was standing over me, holding on to the overhead rail and smiling. I thought to myself, *Isn't everybody a Christian?*

I replied yes very softly. She was perky and still smiling. I continued reading. She bubbled out again, "What church do you go to?" Gosh, I thought, she is going to expose me on the bus. Church? I thought. I have not been to church in over twenty years. I just wanted her to shut up with her boldness, so I softly said, "No church, I am not going to church now."

She replied, "Would you like to go to church with me?"

I said, "What Church." She told me the name of a Baptist church. I thought to myself, *jeeps* BAPTIST*! No way! I am Catholic*" I could not believe she could be so bold; she openly invited me to church on the bus!

I decided well, only maids and lower class people whom I knew of in Jamaica went to the Baptist church, and they were so loud. I told her I would consider it. She gave me her name and number. Would you believe that later in my walk with the Lord, she was like a gentle sweet lamb, compared to my loud boldness? I was so excited in my *new life*, I was like a lion going after souls. Especially after I became a certified evangelist.

Whether you want to believe this or not, it is up to you, but since the day of my confession, I started talking to God like I talked to a human being standing before me. I talked with him one on one. However, my confession that I had at home, to me, was a sort of: "If you do this for me I will do that for you, dear God."

After canceling out with her two Sundays in a row because I did not want to go to the Baptist church. One day, I was walking away from the phone after talking to her and I literally heard a voice say, "You want to go to church or not?" I looked around. No one was there, suddenly a fear struck me; I did not want to be hit down again. I said, "Okay, God, if you really want me to go to the Baptist church, I will go." I turned around, went back to the phone and called her.

I started going to the Baptist church with her, I think, October 1979. Here comes my open acknowledging part. I noticed in the Baptist church that after every service, they would give an altar call, and this would rock my brains Sunday after Sunday. It reminded me that as a child my mother would send us to Sunday morning services at the Methodist church, up the street from our home, because it was within walking distance for us. Then in the evenings, we would go with her to our church, Holy Trinity Catholic church. I was always in awe over this church. In any event, the Methodist church would have from time to time something called Synods in large open areas. As children, we were pooled to these Synods, and I remember when they made these altar calls, I always wanted to go forward but would fight from doing so, as I would be too embarrassed for my friends or anyone, as a matter of fact, in that big congregation to see me going forward, so I would just stand where I was and cry, trying my best not to let anyone see me crying.

However, every Sunday in this Baptist church where I was now attending, they would give this altar call. I now know as "open confession," whereas, in the Catholic Church, we call it "closed confession."

One particular Christmas Sunday, our Bible study teacher in our singles class was teaching and preaching, he said, "You see, accepting Jesus is like driving on the highway and you see an exit, which you meant to take, but you say, 'Oh, never mind, I will take the other one,' then you come to the other exit and you say again, 'Oh, I will take the other one.' But you never take it, you keep postponing exits until it is too late, you meet with an accident and it is too late, you never get off the highway." I never looked at it that way before. I kept wanting to accept Jesus as my Lord and Savior publicly but never doing it. I was always saying, "Next week I will go forward," "Next week I will go forward," but I never seemed to get the nerve to do it.

Bible studies were over. We proceeded to the main church for morning service. The service was beautiful. Our pastor took the ball that our Bible teacher had started rolling and hit the ball straight into my heart. It exploded into thousands of pieces. I stood there thinking I was going to faint, but the funny part about it was, when I thought I was going to faint, I felt lighter than I was the day after my confession.

I remember the pastor vividly saying, "What better time to accept Christ as your Savior than at the time of his birth? He's coming as a baby for you, yet you still deny him, Jesus says if you profess me before men, I will profess you before my Father, if you deny me, I will deny you." I mean, that did it! My heart was pounding so hard, I was sure it was going to burst, tears were running down my face. Mascara, eye shadow, and all, I was so nervous I had to hold tight to the railing of the pew before me. I did not know what to do.

I wanted to go forward but I kept saying what if my skirt fell off, what if my shoe heel broke, what if, what if. Then all of a sudden, I shook my head, hissed my teeth then said to the lady beside me, "Excuse me." The next thing I knew I was walking down the aisle to the altar. I will never forget that day as long as I live. The minute, the minute I started walking I became calm, steady, and relaxed. I did not understand it at all, but I reached the altar safely. My skirt did not fall off, my heel did not break. No shaking, just peace. Later, I learned it is called "peaceful surrender." The pastor asked me if I had accepted Christ as my Savior, and I said yes. He asked where, I said at home. He asked me if I wanted to be baptized, I said yes.

I had such a clean feeling, which stayed with me for days. I started getting used to this feeling. Now, I know better, of course, especially when I listen to preachers asking if you have the Holy Spirit within you, and talking about the symptoms of the Holy Spirit.

Well, that takes care of my confession and my acknowledging. Now to my submersed baptism.

One Sunday morning in March 1980, I was baptized. Incidentally, when I returned to the Catholic Church, I understood that I did not need to be submersed since I was already baptized as an infant. That's how green I was. Now, however, as far as I am concerned—doesn't matter—twice is better than zero. I started growing stronger and stronger in faith, stronger and stronger in love with my God and Savior.

I discovered that the things I used to enjoy doing, did not appeal to me anymore. This was not because I had been trying to fight or avoid doing them. Instead, it was just that my entire structure had changed since Jesus came to live inside me. I truly had no desires for the things I once desired, for the things I once wanted, because I wanted them no more. I went into celibacy for years.

I have come a long, long way up this road to Jesus. Everything, everything I desire, I talk to the Holy Spirit about. I ask the Holy Spirit for Christian friends, I get them, Christian functions, I get them, answers to questions, I get them. This part is real scary. I go to sleep at nights, my lips are not moving, yet I am singing loud and clear. I hear myself singing throughout the house, yet my lips are closed, Singing and praising God. I wake up in the morning and the same thing is going on inside of me. The change over me is magnificent.

I thank God for everything. I talk to him about everything. Now, I am asking his Holy Spirit to use me in whatever manner he wants to and never, ever, let me go. I know I truly am born-again! I do look forward to living my life, walking with God.

Amen, Amen, and Amen
Elnieda Telfer-Sinclair
December 1980

Born-again? Yes, because everything becomes new as a new born child. Your perspectives in life change. You become a new person in him.

You may ask "second life?" My answer to that is…yes, my brothers and sisters, there is a first life, Bc (before Christ), and a second life, Ad (after Christ).

At age 39, Lunchtime- Secretary, Hotel
Inter*Continental Miami, Florida

My New Life

To Being Born-again Life Took on a New Meaning for Me

My brothers and sisters, God was going to use my youngest child, a son he had given me to draw me closer to him, but I did not know this. You see, soon after I moved into my dream home, he started going to a charismatic prayer service held in the Sheraton Hotel. The hotel was in our backyard, so to speak.

There were times when he would be under his bed praying for me. I knew he was, because he would confront me about my lifestyle, going on all these dates and partying, but I would just ignore him. Under his bed was his prayer closet.

By this time, I was living in Miami; he had stayed in Jamaica. He was calling me daily from Jamaica, telling me he was now ready to come to Miami. Eventually, I took a weekend and went to Jamaica for him. Luckily, I had processed all his papers before leaving the Island.

He was always a rebellious child, wanting everything his way. Ever since I can remember, he was rebellious. I thought to myself, *He is young. He will outgrow his rebellious attitudes.* Things would change as time would go by, and he would grow older. My other children insisted that I spoilt him because he was the baby.

Yes, of course, he did change, but for the worse because his childish rebellions became teenage rebellions moving into a young man's rebellion. *What was he rebelling about?* I asked myself. I worked two full-time jobs to provide for us. I gave them everything I could. They were never hungry. They lived in one of the best homes in our neighborhood.

What more could I do? What more did they expect from me?

Later in life, I realized that he needed a father. Not having a father did not affect my other two children as much as it affected him. I never knew the impact of a divorce because I grew up in a fun home. Perhaps if I had the time to actually have a daily walk, talk, relationship with *our* Heavenly Father, then I would have been able to sit and talk with my children and instill in them that they *had* a *Father*, a Heavenly *Father.* This I did not know. In my little mind, I thought God was way, way, up there in the heavens with lots to do, and little me was way, way, down here to fight for my life and survival on my own. If I did not struggle and fight who was going to take care of me and my children? If I knew then, what I know now, life could have been so much sweeter, better, and smoother. I would have saved myself tremendous grief.

Did I know that the man who fathered them on earth also needed a *Father?* Did I know that *he* is the *Father* of us all? Did I know that the scripture says that *our Father* is going to ask us one day, "*What have you done with the children I gave you?* Did I know that the scripture says, "*You have made* MY *children go a whoring?* What? What is God talking about? I thought they were my children...No, my brothers and sisters, I knew nothing about this. Did I think that the dictionary was given to us for spelling knowledge? Did I think that the map was given to us for directions? Did I think that the Word of God, the Bible, was given to us to teach us about life and how to live? No, my brothers and sisters, we don't stop to *think* about these things.

Now I look back and I know that, *If it was not for the Lord on my side...* He certainly heard and answered prayers that went up for me. Thank you, Lord!

I had my born-again experience on a Saturday morning at home and was able to survive the weekend, but Monday was a-coming. On Monday, I had to go to work. I was still in a trance. Walking to work from the bus stop was a drama in itself because that light feathery feeling I felt from Saturday was still all over my being.

Suddenly I became confused because I was feeling so light. I found myself walking, looking down on my body, touching my body, thinking, *Did I put my girdle on? Do I have my stockings on? Why am I feeling so light? Would the wind from the ocean blow me away?* all these thoughts. Then I realized, I was on Brickell Avenue; Brickell is equivalent to Park Avenue, New York. I was now working at the Hotel Intercontinental Miami, as secretary to the director of marketing, so I quickly looked up and walked as fast as I could to the office.

Surprise, Surprise! I was almost blown away, as I entered the office, because two of my friends and coworkers were there before I arrived. They looked at me and said, "What happened to you?"

I said, "Nothing."

They said, "You're sure? You look different...." I smiled and went to my desk. Evening came. It was time for happy hour in our pub, Pete's Pub. Two of my girlfriends came to get me. When I started working at the hotel there were three girls who were good friends. They were called The Three Musketeers. After my arrival, I became friends with them. The name was changed to "The Three Musketeers, Plus One," I was the "one." I said to them, "No, I am not going to happy hour today."

They asked why.

I don't remember what I said, but whatever excuse I gave them, they accepted and said, "Tomorrow."

Of course, tomorrow came. Once again they came to get me, as they usually did. I said, "No, I do not want to go."

They said in unison, "WHAT! Two days in a row? Are you kidding? Come on. Tell us what happened, something happened. We know, tell us."

I was very reluctant to tell them because I was afraid they would laugh at me, but they were persistent, so I told them everything, ending with the note that I cursed God, asked if he was real; he came into my apartment, and knocked me out. I got up changed.

I can still see their faces, as they listened, then one said, "Wow! Tootsie, you are serious!"

Another one said, "That is so beautiful!" You could hear a pin drop; the office was so quiet. They got up slowly and left. I went home. No one asked me to happy hour again, and I never went.

I knew something was also going on with me, but I did not know what it was. All I knew was, the things I used to do, I no longer wanted to do.

The places I used to go, I no longer wanted to go. I just wanted to go home and read the Bible. I read the Bible from Genesis to Revelation twice. I then read the New Testament thrice. When that was not enough for me, I began typing the Bible on my typewriter, translating it into my my everyday simple words. Later I found out that there were many modern day translations, but I still keep and will always keep mine because to me it is so simple.

Bible Studies

For seven years, during my lunch time, I attended Bible studies at the Presbyterian church on Brickell Avenue. I was hungry for the Word of God. I grew in leaps and bounds in his kingdom, spreading my wings as far as he allowed me.

My brothers and sisters, once God touches you and turns your life around, you have no choice but to go forward, wherever he leads you. That's what it means to be born-again.

Born-again because everything becomes new. Your perspectives in life change. You become a new person in him. I was born on the Island of Jamaica where everything moves at a slow pace. You will always hear words like: "Take it easy," "Soon come," "Wait, man," etc. Like anyone else, you and I, we dream of faraway places; we desire finer things; we want more; we aim for the best, so we head out in life to achieve our dreams.

We move to metropolitan cities, move to another country; we enter the world of hustle and bustle; we work till we sometimes drop. We acquire, we achieve, we accumulate, we have excess. So we store. Then we download, we sell, we give away, we throw out.

Then we become worn out, beaten down, tired to the max. So we give away, we downsize. Then we look for a quiet, simple place to relax, to think, "What's the hurry?" "Wait a minute." "Relax." "What the heck was it all about?" etc.

It takes us back to our childhood, *then* we realize the circle of life, yet, through it all we appreciate the fact that *life* is wonderful, *life* is for living, *life* is great... *but* only if we live it in order to answer to the Creator of Life, our God... failing that, we continue with wasted years, wasting our lives going nowhere. Some going nowhere fast, some going nowhere slowly. Truth is, we end up somewhere.

The best part of life is, that we have the choice to choose where we are going, where we want to go. Personally, I have decided to go back to the Father from whence I came, my God. God the Father in the person of my Lord Jesus Christ. God the Father who is present here with us in the form of his Blessed Holy Spirit. I can only thank him that I have lived long enough and was blessed to come to the realization that *life* is a journey.

I have accepted *the way* of that journey. In this journey, I have found out that God is with us in ways we never imagined or dreamed of in our wildest dreams, asking us to completely surrender our all to him. Not easy. Ask me. I will tell you. Perfect, heck no! Ask me. I will tell you. I usually sing, "Amazing Grace how sweet the sound that saved a *bitch* like me." (Yes, the correct word is *wretch*, but it sounds too mild for me compared to the bitch life had turned me into, so if it is not a bother to you, I would like that word to stay. You will see why, 2 chapters down). Trust me, I have a *new life.* I had a boyfriend once who said to me, "Tootsie, please promise me one thing, if we ever break up, please let us remain friends because I would never want you as an enemy." He is still alive and well. I hope he will read this book as I will let him know that I have written a book.

Since my conversion, there have been times in my life when God has taken me into places to be used by him, which I could only pause in utter shock that unworthy as I am, he would see fit to use me, this garbage can that he had cleaned up, to touch and change the lives of others.

My brothers and sisters, please listen to me, DO NOT allow the bitterness, anger, and resentment of things done to you—whether present or past—by a member of the opposite sex, whom you love or loved, or by any one family member, religious or otherwise, turn you into a bitch, a bulldog, or an evil person. I came to learn that there are many beautiful, kind, loving, sincere men and women who are completely the opposite of the cruelty we encountered. Ask your Father God to lead you to those people. Bearing in mind, that even when you meet them, it does not mean that he or she is your compatible mate. *But,* never give up. *Know* that, that special person is there *just for you.* At the time of writing this, Tuesday, February 19, 2013, I am still praying for my compatible mate. Please do not tell me that he is not born as yet and his mother is dead because I refuse to believe it. We will love each other regardless of our flaws. We will love each other for who we are. We will not be hot-tempered towards each other. He will be all I ever hoped and prayed for. We will both know that we were meant for each other—if one person knows it and the other does not. It ain't him or her.

Back to my book…

While in these places, where God took me to be used for his glory, I would sometimes look around, tears would fill my eyes, my heart would pound for joy, my feet would move with excitement, but my voice would never quiver. Those were his grace and mercies. All I could do was to look up to him and say wow. From the pit to the palace, I really am royalty.

People would *always* ask me, "Elnieda, you always dress up going to church, why?" My answer would *always* be the same. "If I was invited to Buckingham Palace or the White House, I would dress my best. Now I am going to my Father's house, the palace of the King of kings, shouldn't I not dress appropriately for him? Are you kidding? When I was going on the town, I would purchase new outfits, go to the beauty shop, dress to the hilt only to come out smelling like a smoked pig, not to mention sometimes the headache, that followed from too much smoke in the buildings, and you ask me why I dress up to go to my Father's holy, happy, clean, house? The true palace?"

Needless to say, they got the message. I could easily have said, "Out of respect," without the elaboration, but please don't ask me questions if you are not ready for my answers.

Places the Lord Has Taken Me

Veterans Hospital; Miami, Florida.

I was born-again at home. The Lord led me into the Baptist church…I stayed in that church for over two years. While there, I was taught and studied the Word of God—the Bible. I grew in leaps and bounds. I was hungry for the Word. I was on fire for The Lord. The Bible taught me *everything* about life. How to live; why we live. How to love;

why we love. How to share; why we share. How to talk with him, my Heavenly Father, etc., so while studying the Word, I was led to volunteering, to give back. I chose to give back to the men and women who wore a uniform to represent and serve this country, the United States of America, who fought and died for it, so I could have the privilege of living here. I decided to volunteer at the Veterans Hospital since the Veterans kept the doors open for me.

More about this in my chapter, "Seasons of my life."

As God would have it, my two sons served in the military. Christopher, four years in the Navy as of today, (September 25, 2014, Wade is still in the service for almost 26 years. He served two terms in Iraq and one term in Afghanistan where he was wounded three weeks after arriving there. God willing, he retires from the Air Force in 2015). Praise be to God, now and forever.

I worked as a legal secretary for eleven years in Miami. On Saturdays, I would go to the Veterans Hospital. I had the privilege of working on two floors, the ninth and the eleventh. That, my brothers and sisters, is a book by itself. The wonderful people I met there, the joys and sorrows of working there; the blessings I received working there.

I volunteered 750 hours.

America for Jesus

This was held in Orlando, Florida. I went with some of my friends from the Baptist church . It was a tent pitching camp rally. This was the first time I slept/lived in a tent.

After two days of this tent, I shouted, "Where is the nearest Holiday Inn?" I checked into the nearest hotel. Not to worry, my physical experience was nothing compared to the spiritual experiences I had with God at this rally. It was the push start I needed to "go and tell."

March in Overtown—Miami, Florida

I had moved from Dadeland in the Southwest to Brickell Avenue downtown. By now I had found and was hooked on TBN (Trinity Broadcasting Corporation), a twenty-four-hour Christian network. One night they announced that this man who walks around the world with a cross was coming to Miami to walk through Overtown with the cross. About a month or so earlier, Overtown had endured a very bad riot over a racial shoot-out and the killing of a young black man by the police. Many people were killed. The town was almost completely destroyed by rioting and fires set by the angry crowd. Since I was now living near Coconut Grove, I decided to go and participate in this march from the Grove to Overtown. That was something I would never ever have done and will never forget. Me in a march behind a cross? Never!

At that march, I met a woman who became one of my dearest friends. She has since gone to be with the Lord. She told me she attended Coconut Grove Baptist Church. She invited me to their Thursday night prayer meeting. I went.

Shock of my life. I had never attended a prayer meeting before, *and* even more deadly, *this was a charismatic prayer meeting.* I thought to myself, *These people are all crazy, why are they singing so loudly? Lifting their hands? Dancing? Clapping? Now I died, what language are they talking? Wait a minute, every one is talking in another language, let me out of here.* I was scared out of my wits. I was even more scared to leave because I was way up in the second pew. *Oh, Lord,* I thought, *I am never ever coming back to this church.*

Weak from all their carryings-on and my being tense and afraid, I could not leave because I thought they would tackle me. I just slumped down in my seat and closed my eyes. Talk about something coming over me! Know that song? Well yep! Something did come over me after I closed my eyes. The screaming voices, the clapping, the loud music, everything sounded sweetly in my ears. It seemed as if I was in another world. My entire being relaxed and the tears came rolling down my face. All because I was listening, not looking and criticizing.

Needless to say I went back again and again, and the preaching and teaching from the Word was awesome. One day, the pastor reminded the meeting that this coming Sunday was the Prison Ministry Sunday. They would be meeting at the Stockade at 10:00 a.m. Of course, by now I was more than on fire for the Lord so I got directions and showed up for duty. I had no intention of missing *anything.*

Dade County Stockade—Miami, Florida

Unforgettable! Absolutely unforgettable experiences too many to mention here. I learned that prisoners were humans. Prisoners were someone's little adorable baby, prisoners had dreams like everyone else, not all prisoners were bad people, that sometimes prisoners were in prison because of circumstances, some by choice, some by mistakes, some by bad influences, some by dire need, etc. Eventually, to me, it boiled down to the fact that I, another person, could be in here also, as a prisoner, *but by the Grace of God, I was on the outside.*

The Prison Ministries have taught me to respect the human race whoever and wherever they are, and not to judge because one day we will all meet the *judge.* When I talked to these men and women, many times I would say to myself, *Lord have mercy on judges who had to make these decisions, that is one job I would never want to do. Please give them the wisdom of King Solomon.*

Different Churches

I was now going to many different churches, attending Christian concerts and functions but still maintaining the Baptist church as my home church. At church, I started asking questions about the churches I attended. Questions such as why do this or that church raise their hands when they sing in such a sweet surrender attitude and this or that church don't? I heard about the Paraclete as a child in the Catholic Church but this or that church never mentions it, why? I always thought of it as a big bird and was afraid it would pick me up one day when I did wrong. Why didn't this or that church fast? Why did only some churches sing in tongues? etc. I know now that these are no-no questions for the Baptists. Anyway, the answers given to me were never fulfilling. *But* one day I might turn on the radio or the TV, or open the Word and I would hear a preacher talking about the Paraclete. I would learn that it was not a big bad bird, instead it was a form of the blessed Holy Spirit, or one day I would open the Word and I would learn why we fast and pray, etc. Therefore, I started searching the scriptures for myself and the scriptures answered all my questions. My greatest discovery was that the nuns were not wrong at all, that they were not super theologians sent to baby spoon-feed us; they had a divine calling and decided to follow Jesus. In so doing, they taught us from their hearts. Be it wrong or right. It was then up to us to seek and find him for ourselves to grow in faith and knowledge. It turned out, my brothers and sisters, that the Bible taught me more about the Catholic Church than the Catholic Church taught me about the Catholic Church.

St. Louis Catholic Church

While working at the law firm, I went on vacation. When I returned to work and entered my cubicle, I saw a note on my desk saying, "Hello sister, I had the pleasure of working at your desk, and I realized you are a sister in Christ. It was a joy just being here. If the Spirit leads you, please give me a call, so we can fellowship together." I called her. We decided to meet one Sunday morning for church. She attended the Presbyterian Church. I had heard her pastor on the radio several times. I waited at my gate for her then I saw this smiling, lovely young blond woman pulling up beside me. We had a wonderful fellowship that day and became great friends. We visited many churches, retreats, functions, and single groups together.

One day she called me very excited. She said "Elnieda, I know your heart is in the Catholic Church and guess what? Last night I went to this Catholic church in the southwest. It blew me away. You just have to go and visit."

I said to her, "Nancy, you must be crazy, you know I want to leave the Baptist church because I need more, *but* a Catholic church? That's like jumping from the frying pan into the water. I want fire. What are they going to teach me that I don't know already?" That was the end of that.

A few days after she told me about this church, I was driving up US1 and I saw a car with a bumper sticker with the words: "The Lord Be With You, St. Louis Catholic church." I thought to myself, *What Catholic church would be so bold as to have a bumper sticker like that,* the Catholic

Church was so laid back. I forgot about it. Would you believe this? After that, almost everywhere I went, I saw this bumper sticker. I started thinking, *Lord, are you trying to tell me something?*

About a year or so later, I decided to move from Brickell to Kendall in the southwest. I needed a less expensive place. I moved into Four Quarters Habitat.

This is not the end of this bumper-sticker phenomenon, but just the beginning. I tell you, God will hit you over the head with iron or paper, take your choice, anything to get your attention.

Coming from work two days after I moved in, I drove into my parking space. You guessed it; the car in the designated space beside me had the bumper sticker. I said, this is it, the Lord is speaking. Just to be sure, I went inside picked up the phone and called my girlfriend. I asked her, "What is the name of that Catholic church you told me about sometime ago?"

She said, "St. Louis Catholic Church."

I said to her, "I have been seeing cars with these St. Louis bumper stickers since you told me about that church and guess what? The car in the parking space beside mine has it also." We both laughed at this. I told her I was going to look out for the person who drove that car and find out where the church is located.

One evening as I drove in, I saw a gentleman washing the car. I believed I scared him because I hurriedly parked, jumped out of the car, and rushed to him, asking, "You go to that church?" Stunned, he looked at me with his eyes popping, (he was very handsome with the most beautiful blue eyes you ever saw) holding his sponge, he softly said yes.

Steve and Linda Melus came into my life

I blurted, "Can I come?"

He replied, "Let me ask my wife," I knew he wanted to run, so I did not move, he had to come back to his car. He came back with his wife all right, and she said, "As a matter of fact, we are going there tonight to our Thursday night prayer meeting. If you want, you can come with us."

If I wanted? This beautiful couple came into my life. Life is never dull when you really know how to live with God. He truly brings excitement and vigor into your body, soul and spirit. He brings a clean, safe, happy enjoyment with cheerful, caring, self-giving friends.

The prayer meeting was held at night. The grounds were not lit, so I could not see the main church building. I did see some sort of a building that looked like a flying saucer, but we went behind it into the social hall where the meeting was being held. I sat in amazement. I could not believe I was at a *Catholic prayer meeting* because I was experiencing the same atmosphere that I experienced at the Coconut Grove Baptist church's prayer meeting and at the home of some believing Jews who worshipped Jesus, their Y'suha, in Yiddish, years ago. Back then during my search for a church, I had visited a prayer meeting consisting of Jews who accepted Jesus as Lord and became Christians. They had a prayer meeting every Monday night. While they were praying and worshiping Jesus in Yiddish and calling out to Y'shua, I felt as if I was in Israel in the days of old, and I knew Jesus was there. I felt as if I was a part of old Israel. I basked in ecstasy for Y'shua. The feeling was a feeling I had never felt before.

Back to the St. Louis prayer meeting. I felt sorry for this sweet, dear, gentle couple because they could not concentrate on the meeting. I kept bothering them. Eventually, they just decided to forget it and focus on helping me comprehend that it was a Catholic church . Finally, the last time I poked the wife and asked, "Are you *sure* this is a Catholic church?" She gave up and said, "Yes, it is, tell you what. Why don't you just come to Mass on Sunday and see for yourself." I said okay.

The Mass

Sundays, I normally went to the 11:00 a.m. service at the Baptist church. This Sunday, however, I decided, to go to the 9:30 Mass, which ended at 10:30. That would give me time to go to the Baptist church at 11:00. Just in case I was not "spiritually receiving" anything from St. Louis, I would still have a church home. On Sunday morning I got dressed. I was going downstairs to leave for St. Louis when I heard the Lord speak to me in that gentle inner voice, "You are going to church?" I kept walking and said, "Yes, I am going to church."

He said, "Take your Bible."

I said, "Bible? No one takes a Bible to the Catholic Church, the Priests read from the Bible." I kept walking.

I heard again, "Take your Bible." I got the message, no more slapping down for me. I ran back, went upstairs, grabbed my Bible and left.

It was not until I reached the church grounds that I realized I did not grab my standard Bible. Instead, I had grabbed the large Bible. I saw no one else with a Bible. All of a sudden, I felt awkward with this huge Bible, but I just walked in with it.

I entered the sanctuary through the second entrance. As I entered, I turned my head towards the congregation and looked around, it was packed, with standing room only. A feeling of pride, love, peace and joy swept all over me. Suddenly I just knew this was "*IT.*" Long, long before the Mass began, I knew this was "it." I felt *pride* that the Catholic Church was still alive and well. *Love* because as a child I had always loved the Catholic Church. It was only during my struggles in life that I forgot and left it, especially since I was so bored with it during my teenage years. *Peace* because I knew this was where I belonged, and *joy* because I had finally found what I was searching for. I rested my head on the wall of the church and said, "Thank you, Lord, I am home!" The Mass began.

Father Russell was the priest. He was reading the Gospel, all of a sudden he stopped and read it again then he shouted, "I don't like this version, there is another version that I like, who has a Bible?" A lady closer to him jumped up and gave him a Bible. I said to myself, *Yeah, yeah, they carry the Bible*. I came alive. I cried. I sang with them, clapped with them, and I praised God with them. I knew without a shadow of doubt that I had been in the presence of the Lord, and that I wanted to be in St. Louis Catholic church. I wanted to return home.

My new friends who took me to the prayer meeting had told me about this Father Russell, but since I had neither heard nor seen him, I did not know what to expect. Needless to say, I was taken aback when he entered the church with such zeal. He was jumping, clapping, singing, what a breath of fresh air. The church was alive. Thank God! Father read the Gospel, he actually preached up a storm on the altar. The Mass was more than alive, it was exciting, stimulating, and hitting home. I laughed a little, cried a little. I remember jumping and skipping back to my car with butterflies inside of me. I ran into my Baptist church to tell the exciting news about St. Louis. They were not excited.

It so happened, for this particular Sunday the pastor had previously announced that he wanted the entire congregation inside the main church because he needed to talk to them before the service. I was in time for his talk. I was praying, "Oh God, please show me how to leave here, please let me know if I am doing the right thing because these people took me in, cleaned me up, fed me the Word, and now I want to leave." I prayed and prayed.

Then the pastor began. He was saying, "We are a Baptist church, we would like it to be known that we believe in so and so, we are so and so, and we are not going to change. Our teaching is so and so." Some people were asking him questions and he was responding. It was beginning to get heated and quickly turning into a debating session.

I stood up and said, "Pastor, I am so glad you just said what you said, because I had a very serious decision to make as to my future in this church and you just helped me to make my decision. Thank you." I sat down. A wonderful pastor, a man of God in every way, who was visiting that Sunday morning stood up and said, "Maybe these questions and answers should be postponed until a Wednesday night meeting in order for us to continue with the worship services." Thank God, that stopped the tempers from flying and moved us into the services. I knew I was going to leave. I knew I had to tell them, but I was so angry with the pastor for the things he had said, that I was not going to go back and say goodbye, I was just going to leave. That was it.

However, when I went home, I called one of the members, a dear brother in the Lord, with an equally precious wife, and told him how angry I was, etc. He listened to my griping then he said to me, "I understand how you feel Elnieda, but you still have to love. You have to do what you have to do the proper way and you must forgive." I knew what he was telling me was the truth, he calmed me down.

I decided to go back to the Sunday night service and say goodbye properly. I got dressed, but before going to church, I was so nervous that I decided to pass by the home of my newfound Catholic friends, let them know that I went to Mass as they suggested, and about my decision to say goodbye to my Baptist church members. I told them that I was going to join St. Louis.

It so happened that when I was there, they had a visitor from St. Louis, they all decided to lay hands on me and pray for me before I left. That did it. I have never encountered anyone laying hands on me and praying for me. I received all the peace, strength, and assurance that I needed. I reached the church late, but I was actually happy and smiling. After the evening service, I hugged almost everyone I could, kissed them, told them thanks for everything, how much I loved them, told them goodbye. Of course the majority of them were shocked. My singles group expected it, so they were not at all surprised. They said they knew from the minute I spoke in church that morning what my decision would be. Some told me the exact thing, I had thought to myself some time ago. "Elnieda, you are jumping from the frying pan to the fire."

Did I?

We have a God so big and so wonderful; HE IS AMAZING. Amazing not only in his grace but in everything.

In 1984, I became a member of St. Louis Catholic Church. I had no idea the church was that huge. It had eighteen thousand members with over a hundred ministries. Here I grew daily in leaps and bounds, becoming more and more involved in the charismatic movement. I was involved in evangelization, home groups, the ministry of the Eucharist, prison ministry, prayer meetings, retreats, etc. The first retreat I made at St. Louis was the *Emmaus retreat.* This was a weekend retreat. I cried all that weekend and left there a new person. Later on, I attended the Life in the Spirit Seminar.

The Life in the Spirit Seminar

This seminar turned out to be the beginning of a series of seminars, leading and giving me the privilege and opportunity to become a speaker. I used to sit in these seminars and listen with amazement to the speakers talk about their lives before Christ, and I knew I was in a safe place, that I was not alone, that God takes garbage cans like me, cleans me up, then he stores fine china and crystal in me and puts me to use. He uses us for his Glory. From time to time, he allows us to show or display the china and crystal so others so others can see them. I often wondered, *What would people think of me if they heard my testimony?* I never dreamt that one day I would be asked to be a speaker.

Some years later, the leaders or facilitators of the seminar were passing the mantle to new leaders. The new leaders, to my surprise, asked me to be a co-leader of one of the groups for the next Seminar. They, no one in the church, knew anything about me, especially my testimony. Many seminars followed. I then became a group leader. Years passed. These facilitators moved to another state.

The next leader or facilitator asked me to be a speaker in addition to being a group leader. My talk would be on salvation. Can God turn the tables? Yes, he can!

As the years went by, God used me to give over sixty talks, three times per year, through St. Louis Catholic Church and other churches, in the women's prison and men's prison.

I was also privileged to attend the Cursillo Retreat.

On 1984 and 1985, St. Louis sent the head of the pastoral council, the church secretary, one of our cantors, and myself to attend the the Evangelization Explosion seminar in Fort Lauderdale for training in evangelizing.

This took me to a new level of how to present the gospel to others. I always knew I needed training because there were many times when people asked me about the Lord Jesus, and I would go on and on about how wonderful he was, how he changed my life, etc., but not really understanding how to present him—the God Man—to them in a more intelligent manner. This ministry was very exciting and an eye opener for me. I soon realized that one should never ever take another person's faith for granted, or judge them as to who was holier than who, or, just because they don't praise as openly as you do, that their faith or love of God is less than yours.

This ministry gave me rude awakenings. I learned to be sensitive, not to judge others based off what I saw on the outside. I learned that just because we see people walking or acting like they have halos on their heads, or as if they have it all together, all the time, does not necessarily mean that they do.

That the ones who we think do not have the halos are the ones who actually may have the halos. I say that to say this.

I never said the rosary. That's another saga by itself. I was born-again. God slapped me down, so I could look up. Not Mother Mary. Hence, I refused to say the rosary. So, basically, in my tiny mind, once again, I intended to go after mostly those devoted people praying the rosaries because I thought, *They need to know that Jesus saves them, not Mother Mary.* Now, can you believe this? Me, coming from a life of sin, could believe that I was flying so high because I was saved by his Grace and had decided to attack people with scriptures? Those people who had been attending church had been paying the bills, keeping the church open for sinners like me to have a place to come and worship when "the cat is dragged in"—so to speak. And I had the audacity to think that I was going to target these little old ladies before they die to tell them who was their Savior? Well, I got rude awakenings, all right.

I remember the first time I went to this lady and asked her, "If you were to die today and stand before God, and he asked you, 'Why should I let you into my kingdom,' what would you say to him?" with her rosary still in her hand, she said very softly. "I don't know, I guess he would have to ask Jesus because he died for me." *Bang!! I was floored.* Served me right!!

Did I stop? No way! I was on a mission, so time after time, I would approach those who I thought, needed to know, only to be told, *"Don't know, Jesus saves"* or, I would always get," "Jesus will tell him," or "I didn't do anything to deserve it, Jesus knows," etc.

I finally gave up on the people I targeted because I was looking for something negative from them, only to receive positive answers. I decided to take my sad self to the Charismatic prayer meetings where it would be easier, I wouldn't have to judge as everyone would already be super positive. Shock attack again. You know what I got? You guessed it! "I am a good person, at least I try to be" or "I love God" or "I don't kill, steal or do bad things." Hello!!! I did not ask you about good works, which follow salvation and love. I got *nothing, nothing* at all about, "Jesus did it all," "I owe it all to him," "It was by grace," nothing. I was so frustrated; I took these complaints to the next evangelization meeting. I thought they were going to be just as frustrated as I. Instead the leaders only smiled, especially the late Jim Lamb. Jim said, "You see, Elnieda, we never know. That is why we should present the gospel to not just a selected few or to those who we think need it—but to all—because God and God alone knows the hearts of men." I said and will continue to say, Amen to that!

Camillus House—Miami, Florida

While working as a legal secretary, I would notice that after every meeting they had in the conference room, there would be large amounts of left-over bagels, pastries, and sandwiches. Even after members of staff would take for themselves, there would still be leftovers. The firm had two butlers. One day I approached one of them and asked what they did with the leftovers. He said they threw them out. I asked if I could take them, he said yes. I asked him to please don't throw out the platters; I need to arrange them neatly and take them in the platters to the homeless sitting outside Camillus House. He said fine and did exactly as I asked.

Camillus House is a Catholic place of refuge in Miami where the homeless are provided with food, shelter, and medical care. However, if the people did not start lining up outside on the sidewalk from noon or thereabouts, by the time evening came, the beds would all be accounted for and those remaining would have to sleep outside.

After my lunchtime Bible class teacher had left Miami, I had started using that lunch hour to do secretarial work for Brother Paul who was in charge of Camillus House. I would see the men sitting outside hungry and tired waiting for dinner time, while all this expensive good food was going to waste. I started taking the platters and handing out the food to them, going inside, doing my volunteering with Brother Paul, then returning to the office.

Prison Ministries

These were the last ministries I did at St. Louis because in 1990 both my hands collapsed with Carpal Tunnel Syndrome. After thirty-three years of typing, I could no longer type for a living, so after much prayers, the Lord directed me to open a photocopy business, wherein the machines would work for my hands. After he gave me this business, located on the same Brickell Avenue where I worked for eleven years as a secretary, I named it Trinity Copying Services, "Trinity." Five years later, I reorganized the company merging it into the world of digital and graphics, naming it Trinity Graphics & Copy Center, Inc. "Trinity." Trinity is a saga in itself.

Friends of the Good Shepherd

In 1992, the Lord led me to form a non profit corporation, Friends of the Good Shepherd, to assist with the building of "The Church of The Good Shepherd" in Bridgeport, St. Catherine, Jamaica.

At age 43, Family Member's Book, St. Louis
Catholic Church, Miami, Florida

At age 50, Law Firm of Blackwell Walker, Miami, Florida

At age 56, Family Member's Book, St. Louis
Catholic Church, Miami, Florida

Seasons of My Life

The Villages, FL 32163

I spoke with someone on Saturday night who was once an active member in our church, St. Louis Catholic Church. I heard he had recently left the church, but I gave no thought to it. However, another friend called me on Saturday asking me to call this person and ask him why he had left the church. I did. What he told me did not at all bother me. Instead I was grieved in my spirit and hurt at the same time to hear that in these modern days with the movement of the Holy Spirit, people still attacked and hurt the church.

It was late on Friday night when I spoke with him so I was in bed. After our conversation, I lay there and cried out to God deeply, sincerely, and earnestly. This person said God had told him to leave the church. I know God talks to him, but God also talks to me. God and I converse all the time and I know his voice. I said, "Father God. Before I came back to you, I spoke with you and you answered me, I called to you and you came, I asked if you were there, and you showed me that you were. Now Father God, one more time, one more time, talk to me, talk to me. Please let me know if you have told this person that there is witchcraft and idoltary in the Catholic Church, and if so, what we are supposed to do. Where will we be safe? Father when I was in the world, I was never afraid, now that I am in God's family, I have to be afraid? No way, you will have to guide and protect me. But can you please answer me and let me know why you have told him these things? What are we to do?"

By this time, I was really sobbing. My pillow was soaked with tears. I turned on my back and waited on the Lord. Sure enough, he never failed me. The Lord spoke to me. He said, "Let the evil stay with the good, and I will do the separating." I said, "Oh, my God, you mean in the manner when the servant went to his master and told him that the weeds were growing along with the fruits and asked whether or not he should weed them out, and the master said to him, no, because you might hurt the good trees, harvest is coming, on the day of harvest we will pull them all together and burn the weeds at that time?"

The Lord said yes. I asked, "But why in the church?" He reminded me that in the days of Job, Satan was going to church. That scripture came to my mind. I just cried and laughed and said, "Thank you, Father," and went to sleep with the thought in my head, *let the church be the church.*

I awoke on Sunday morning with peace, forgetting the entire incident. I turned my TV dial to Channel 45, TBN, my usual station, to hear a Baptist minister by the name of James Robison, who came on at 10:00 a.m. every Sunday morning. His sermon went like this.

"The Church is in bondage. We have placed ourselves in bondage to gluttony, slavery, etc. We are continually pointing out the faults in others, we beat each other over the heads, we look for the errors of those in the church instead of talking to them about the righteousness of God's presence. Read Matthew 25:34–40. Jesus is crying over his Body. His Body is so split, we are so far apart, we cannot see God's presence. Water is life, his Life. Hungry! The Church is hungry for the Word of God, which is the Bread of Life.

"Naked," he said. "The church is naked for his righteousness. For years we preachers have gone around the world preaching fire coming down, but fire and the power of God will never come down on us until we are one." He then gave an example of how one day he was at a picnic trying to start a fire, and it just would not light. Then the Lord told him just as the coal was scattered so were his people. If the coal came together, it would light, and if his people came together they would light also. He said, "Jesus told me 'we all need the Body, my Body. I have others who have not bowed down to Babel. You are not the only ones that I have.'" He continued, "We should never doubt the Bible, but for us to say to each other you are wrong because you don't see it as we do, we are killing ourselves." He said he saw Jesus crying because we were killing ourselves. Some of us mocked and rejected the gifts and completely refused them, while others to whom he has given the gifts, to, carried them home in a box, placed the box on a table, and bowed down and idolized it. God help us! We adore the gift and not the giver of the gift. Jesus was crying, crying over his people because we go and worship the person with the gift. Jesus is crying because we are tearing his body apart. Everything we say against each other is tearing his body apart. We have to love each other. It is right to love one another; it is right to forgive one another; it is right to come together with one another."

Brothers and sisters, needless to say, this was just the topping for me. The message was so intense that I decided to send away for the tape. I still have this tape.

This same Sunday, I tuned in at 12:00 noon to the same station for Father John Bertuluchi. I never missed him on Sundays. Would you believe it? Listen to Father John's teaching, he began. "I am a person who believes in the charismatic gifts, etc., but I also believe in the Patrine charisma, which was given to Peter. Matthew 16:13–18. 'Who do you say that I am?' This is a question that Jesus will ask each of us sooner or later.

"Who do you say he is? Simon Peter, who was Jewish, answered this question. We cannot get this revelation until God himself touches us. We have to be open to it and seek it, but God himself will have to touch us. Our Holy Father, Pope John always begins and ends his prayers with the words of exultation that Jesus be lifted up. Jesus Christ called upon Peter to confirm the brethren." Father John went on and on. He also quoted Luke 22: 31–34 and John 21:15. This tape I also sent for. Are you ready for the rest?

Same day, Sunday, I went to the six o'clock evening Mass as usual. Sometimes after Mass, I head for Grace Church. I usually reach there just in time to catch the preaching of the Word. The scripture the preacher read was Matt: 16–18, "Upon this rock... ." Of course, he preached on this topic. All I could do was just sit, smile, and say, "Thank you, Jesus. Thank you, Jesus." (I still say and agree.)

Let the Church Be the Church

Brothers and sisters, regardless of what is being said about us Christians, or what will be said, let us stand firm 'till the race is finished. It will not be for the strong but for those who endure and finish the race. I was away from the church for over twenty years. I was born-again at home in 1979. I started my walk with the Lord in the Baptist church. I thank God for the Baptist church that took me in, cleaned me up, made me read the Bible for myself, so I could know what "saith the Lord," and that he still speaks.

Although I was raised and brought up in the Catholic Church, I never understood much about the church. Maybe it was because I was never taught, I never cared, or I never listened, maybe all of the above. I don't know. All I know is that after I began reading and understanding the Bible in the Baptist church, the Bible taught me more about the Catholic Church than the Catholic Church taught me about the Catholic Church. I understood things so more clearly and saw things much more differently. Before, I remember hundreds of questions would pop into my mind about the Catholic Church, but no one was able to give me adequate answers.

Now, all my questions were being answered by the Bible. His Word says, "If you seek me, you shall find me." There were also times when I would just sit in the Baptist church listening to their preaching and would say to, "So, the Catholic Church was teaching the truth all along."

Looking back, had I known that I would be here writing this, I would have written down all the thoughts I had then, so I could share them with you, but I had no idea.

I, you, we cannot defend the Church. It is God's church; he will do the defending. The gates of hell will not come against it. Idolatry and witchcraft may be in every Church, but so is the Holy Spirit and greater, greater is he in us than he who is in the world. We have read the last page in his Book, we know who wins.

So let the church be the church.

Let's love those who despise us and let's pray for unity in God's church, so his Will, will be done.

I do not ever remember being taught that Jesus was not Lord in the Catholic Church, and if it has faults (every church has), pray for the church, stop tearing it apart. For hundreds of years, people have tried to tear it down, but it lives on, for God's sake it must be doing something (not everything) right.

Under My Church

To date, May 15, 1986, my birthday, at this point in my life, after walking seven years with the Lord, I have had only one major regret. My regret? That I wasted over twenty years in the world. Sometimes I look back, reflect on my past life only to get so angry with myself for those wasted years. Now I wonder, how in heavens name could I have been so blind and lost? Why did I take upon my shoulders the cares of life and tried to carry its burdens all those years? Why didn't I just look up to God earlier? King David said, "I will lift mine eyes up to the Lord from whence cometh my help." I guess I was so busy doing my thing that I did not, and could not, find the time to look up. Thank God that he *made* me look up, placed me in such a corner that I could not look beside me, around me, or beneath me. I had one choice, to *look up*, to him, so he could *lift me up*.

Every time I sing the song, "He pulled me out of the miry clay and set my feet on solid ground..." I sing with such praise and adoration to him not only because I can relate to that song, but I can sing it in praise and thankfulness. So many songs that we sing, I can now relate to. They used to be just words but now they all have meanings to me because I have been there. I also know that he does not want me to look back because he has already erased the past. That all the things I had done were only to teach me and lead me to his saving grace.

I pray that the experiences I have had can be passed on to help others. Whenever I see young people going down the same road I once traveled, I cringe thinking of the heartaches and pain awaiting them, so if I can try, with all my heart, to ward them off that road, I will. I can relate to so many to them. Some have listened, some have not, but I pray that God will continue to use me so that they may all take heed. I thank God for the church he had placed me in—St. Louis Catholic Church— for over twenty years, where I grew up in the Word, and became very involved in doing his will.

My dear family and friends:

Sometime ago, one of my dearest friend came to Miami to spend her vacation with me. While staying with me, she accepted the Lord as her Savior. Since then she has been a committed Christian.

During her visit with me, I shared and discussed with her the many things that had happened to me since walking with the Lord—how the Lord had used, and was using, me tremendously. When I told her some of the things, she was amazed and said that I really should put these things in writing to recapture and share them.

The last thing that happened to me was so tremendously nerve-racking, that I have decided to share it with all of you; it is included in this narrative. But, before you read it, please continue to read this, so that you may know where I am coming from.

I was brought up in church as many Jamaicans have been brought up, but as most of us, I drifted away from the church. In those days to me, church was a mere tradition. I did not know God on a personal level. I was brought up in the Catholic Church, every time they mentioned this Holy Ghost, I would really think of him as a *ghost*. In Jamaica, children were usually scared by grownups telling them ghost stories at nights, so the name *ghost* was scary to me. I also heard about witchcraft and the devil, but I always thought, *Who is the devil?* Neither he nor witchcraft could ever interfere with anyone unless they believed in it.

I further thought that only the unintelligent people in Jamaica would think about such things, especially when maids would discuss the things that happened in the remote country areas. I would just let them know that these things were nonsense. I thought I was leading a "good" life because I did not interfere with anyone, I have always gone out of my way to help others, if I sinned, I sinned against myself, not against anyone. Then I remembered that at a point in my life, when my daughter was a teenager, she would constantly complain that something was in her room at nights preventing her from sleeping. I would get angry with her and tell her to get back to her room as nothing was there.

This went on for days. Finally, I made her sleep in my bedroom with me. When she slept in my bedroom, nothing happened to her. Some nights would pass, so she would return to her room. Then, in the middle of the night, she would run back to my bedroom trembling. We were both getting sleepless nights, so we decided to find and go to a Catholic church in the Independence City area, where we were living, to talk with the priest. We found a priest, told him what was happening, and asked if he would come and bless our home. He did and things quieted down for quite a while. Then it started again. This time, I told her to go to the priest at her school on her lunch break and tell him what had happened. She did and he prayed with her and gave her a blessed rosary to sleep with at nights. She did and nothing happened. She told me one morning, that she was sleeping on her stomach, the rosary was under her, she felt the "thing" coming at her, she quickly turned over, put the rosary on her stomach, and it left. I was not afraid, but I was in awe. I then decided to get my child out of Jamaica—for a while at least. I sent her to visit with my mother who, at that time, was living with my youngest sister and her family in Hempstead, Long Island. I never heard any more complaints from my daughter about this "thing" from that day.

She stayed in New York, eventually moving to California to live with her father. Later she married. One day, to my bewilderment, this is what had happened.

I tell you that God is great, that our struggle and fight is really not against each other but against evil forces that we cannot see (Ephesians 6:12). I have, since my conversion, read the Bible twice. All that I did not understand, I now understand; what I should have lived and experienced all my life, I am now living and experiencing. The cleansing that God has given me daily could not be written in this letter. There would not be enough space. In any event, some of my friends, and indeed most people who may read this book, will not, would not, may not know what I am talking about. Unless, of course, they were also born-again.

After talking with my daughter, I went into my living room, fell to the floor on my face. I cried out to God, I said, "Oh Lord, you could have told me more gently, this is a shock, so many things are being thrown at me." He said he was cleansing me and preparing me; regardless of the past, he has forgiven me. I knew then that my skeletons that were in my closets were being pulled out and thrown away, one at a time, even those that I had forgotten.

You see, the Lord cannot deal with things that are hidden. We have to bring them out to the light before him, confess them to him, because whatever we do in the dark, will come out in the light. As the Scripture says: "Our sins will find us out." Thank, God, he only brings them out one at a time. If they all tumbled out of the closet on us in one force, we would surely be buried under them.

I started thinking how in heaven's name this could have happened to my child. The Lord showed me loud and clear. Some of my friends may not like this, but I have to say it anyway.

I had a friend. A very good friend whom I loved dearly, she passed on sometime ago. I pray for her often. She became the center of my life. If I needed to know anything, I would go to her. If I wanted anything, I would go to her. I did not know God on a personal level then. I did not know that God was there for my every need, so I did not go to him.

My friend was the best card reader in town, she had my respect and love. I really went to read my cards for the fun of it, and to listen to what she had to say. I thought she was super wise. At that time, I did not know the seriousness of doing so. Now I know that Ouija boards, card reading, etc., *are not of God.* Please read Leviticus 19:31. It's also in the Book of Deuteronomy, chapter 28.

After reading this, I said, "Oh God, I feel like a garbage can." Then and there the Lord said to me, "Garbage cans can be cleaned and be useful." I did not know what he meant, for a while I was lost thinking about what he said. Then, I remembered. In Jamaica I had a very unusual garbage can that my girlfriend had given me. No dogs could turn it over because of its tight-fitting lid. Everyone wanted one of these cans.

When I was shipping my things to Miami, I ran out of boxes, and I did not know what to do. Suddenly, my eyes rested on the garbage can. I grabbed the hose, soap, water, and a brush. I scrubbed it so clean; I was able to pack my crystals and dishes in it. I knew they would not be broken because the can was so sturdy.

Now I knew what the Lord meant. I cried and said, "Thank you, Father, I feel like a sparkling garbage can." All I can say is God is good. When he cleanses, he cleanses. Even things that we do not remember to ask forgiveness for, or may not even realize that they were sins, he takes away.

My brothers and sisters:

When we stand before a judge on earth and he finds us guilty, he orders us to pay a fine or serve a sentence. We have to pay the consequences. So it is, when we stand before our earthly biological father, he also punishes us, not because he hates us, but rather, because he loves us. We are disciplined.

One day, when we stand before our Heavenly Father, the judge of all, he already knows that we are guilty and he should punish us; but he will withhold punishment because we repented and asked for forgiveness, our sins were washed away with the precious blood of the one who came to save us, our Savior—the second person of the Trinity—our Lord Jesus who is the Christ. Amen!!

Ever thought about it? God is the only one we cannot stand before and ask for justice because we are all guilty. Before him, we can only ask for mercy.

Hence, when he chastises us it is not meant to harm us but to bring us to repentance. We can spare ourselves such needless pain by following his Word, thus avoiding sinful things that only come to us later in life to haunt us.

God richly bless you all.

Love always,
Elnieda

The attached letter regarding my daughter was sent to Evangelist, Brother Wesley:

Ever since I truly started growing with the Lord, taking him seriously, having a personal relationship with him, I have asked him for everything including discernment.

I have often seen you on TBN and although I rejoiced with those who were healed, laughed with them, cried with them, and prayed with them; I still had a slight doubt as to whether you were really and truly called by God, but I did not say anything. I would only think it. You see, the Lord has personally dealt with me about saying anything against any member of his body and because I was scared of another rebuking from him, I kept quiet about my feelings against you. Instead, I did what I should do, talk to him about you. I said, Lord if he is real. Please show me.

The last time you were here in Florida, my friends drove me over from Miami to see you in Broward. I knew that when the young man with cancer was healed at your meeting, it was real because he said he had a burning. That was exactly how I was healed in the hospital a few years ago when my then pastor prayed over my stomach and that burning came over me.

However, I still had my doubts, so when my friends took me home that night, I told them that I would not go all the way to Broward to see you again because I could see your same healing meeting in my bedroom on TBN—knowing full well that we are told to gather with the body.

Sunday night, August 7, I was in bed on the telephone for a long time. The operator cut into my conversation with an urgent call from my daughter who lives in California. She was crying. I asked her what had happened to her. She said her baby was sick, so she took him to Anaheim Convention to John Wesley. She said you passed her then you turned around, looked at her, and cried out, "Demons!" She was crying so hard she could not continue talking to me. Her husband took the phone from her and explained to me that she probably did not know what happened after that as everything happened so fast. He said she jumped up and was struggling with you, and under your power, she went down on the floor. He said, that you, through the power of the Holy Spirit, cast out demons from her before the entire congregation. The most amazing thing about it was when you said: "Demons, you demons from Jamaica."

Now as far as I am concerned, there is no way you have ever seen my daughter before or know where she was born and grew up.

Needless to say I was in shock. Well, not only will I not say anything about the body of Christ anymore, but I will also not *think* anything about the body. This is what I mean when I say the Lord personally deals with me. This one tops them all. I now cannot wait for you to return to Broward County in Florida. I have already cried out to God for his forgiveness and am now asking for your forgiveness.

Elnieda
8475 S.W. 94th Street
Apartment 223E
Miami, FL 33156

Storms in My Life

The Villages, Florida 32163

The story book says, "And they married and lived happily ever after." Not so for me…Real life actually began for me after I left my parents' home and married, might I add, without their consent.

I say this because although we were never rich, not even middle class, just the average struggling family. We never wanted. Our parents tried in their humble hardworking way to make us comfortable and give us what we needed. My mother was a dressmaker. She would make dresses for us in one day, if need be, so we could look our best for that special occasion.

My father was a sailor. He traveled the world. Most of our lives, he was sailing. We loved him so much that it was always exciting when we knew he was coming home. While he traveled, our mother played both the father and mother role. Even though she was not educated to talk to us intelligently about things of the world, which she herself never really knew, she taught us good from bad, most of the time with the rod instead of communicating verbally. I don't think we ever understood why she was so rigid and strict until we started our own families.

All in all, we had fun as children. We were protected by a mother who was like a "mother hen." Mama would always be giving us advice; when a boy visited the home, she would always get 'vibes' as she called it from them. She would then tell us to keep away from so and so. If we disobeyed her, she would tell them directly not to come around.

I met my husband while attending commercial school. He was handsome. He looked just like Elvis Presley; we were in the Elvis rock and roll era. Mama warned me repeatedly about seeing him, but I just could not see myself living without him. She had to be wrong because he was so gorgeous. We would get into arguments and fights over him, so I started to meet him away from home. He had no intention to stop seeing me either because *we were in love!* Even though he knew that I was having problems with my mother over him, he got so excited the day he bought his first car, he drove to my house to show it to me.

Storm Clouds

When my mother saw him, she got so angry she started to gather rocks to throw at him. I got in the middle of it trying to stop her, so she ran inside, took out all my clothes and threw them on the sidewalk. She was so angry, I knew if she got a hold of me she would have killed me, so I jumped inside the car with him and we drove off.

Looking back on the situation over the years, I realized that this poor guy did not want to get caught up into such a situation and neither did my mother, but as I said before, she did not know how to intelligently communicate with us; hence, we had heated arguments over issues we never agreed on.

I moved in with two girlfriends. After two weeks, I knew I was imposing on them. We decided that since he was paying rent for two places, where I was staying and for himself, it would be better to live together. We thought if we paid one rent it would be better. We found a place. A month later, we got married. Needless to say my mother did not attend the wedding, and she forbade my younger sister to attend. By the way, all this happened when I was eighteen years old. He was twenty.

Storm No. 1

Real life then began. Our marriage went fairly well for the first year, during which time I got pregnant with our first child. I think I became pregnant two weeks after our marriage. We knew nothing about birth control and we were both young and naïve in so many ways.

After the birth of our first child, we started having arguments. Later he would start hitting me. I was too embarrassed to let anyone know, so I pretended that everything was alright. I cannot remember the first time he hit me, but it was continuous.

I became pregnant with our second child. Very soon after the birth of our second child, he was beating me so badly that one Friday evening, the maid we had working for us had to intervene in order to rescue me. Later she and I had a long talk about it. She asked me if I had no one else to go to. I told her only my mother, but I was too embarrassed to let her know because she warned me about him, and I did not listen. She told me to swallow my pride and go home to my mother. The next day, I took the children and went home to my mother. My mother took us in, not in any happy welcoming manner but at least no one was beating me.

Storm no. 2

Very soon, he came looking for me, crying to my mother saying that he would never hit me again. I went home with him because he seemed so sincere. This however, became a song and a dance.

During the next two years I had our third child. By then I had left him ten times. I returned to him most of the times because he came begging and the other times because my mother was just so disgusted having me around with the children that she would go off in a wild tantrum if and when we had an argument.

I could not understand why she was so miserable but now that I have grown children, knowing how hard it was to bring them up, knowing that it would tear up my inside to see one of them waste their young lives, then come home to me with three children, I can truly say, *I understand.*

I encountered fifteen storms in this marriage. Finally one night, I sat down with a friend of the family, who was boarding with my mother at that time, and talked about my future.

Starting Life Again

While he and I talked he said, "Look you have to make a final decision. You cannot live with your husband because he beats you. You cannot live with your mother, because she curses you. You run back to him then the cycle continues.

You will never be able to get rid of this life until you make the decision to be on your own." I thought about it and decided to save and get a place of my own, sink or swim. I rented a three-bedroom house in Harbour View. My sister, who was then working, and her girlfriend moved in with me to help with the expenses.

After one year of this, I realized I was still going nowhere fast, so I decided to try and leave Jamaica, at least for a while, to get a start in life. I was a secretary at a law firm in Kingston. A friend at the firm told me what I should do in order to emigrate to America. And so I did.

Emigration to New York
and Starting Life Again

I wanted to go to New York, but I did not have all the money to fly directly, so I booked from Kingston to Miami. In Miami, I purchased a ticket on the Greyhound Bus bound for New York. I will never forget that ride. I was so tired; I thought I was going to die. I think I traveled three days and two nights on that bus, all the time counting the few dollars I had, eating very scarcely. I reached New York with no money and no place to stay. I knew my ex-husband was living in Brooklyn, so I took a taxi to where he was living, determined to get some money from him to find a place. Since he owed me, by then, three or four years of support for the children. I did not know that in America you must telephone someone before you go to visit. Looking back, I know how blessed I was to find him at home. He told me I could stay there, but he was going to tell his wife that I was his cousin.

A few days later, the bottom to this proposition fell through. His wife, at that time, was pouring her heart out to me about not getting support for her two children from their father. We were all in the kitchen talking, my ex, she, and I.

I felt sorry for her because I knew exactly what she was going through. I knew because the father of my children, her husband, was not supporting our three children either. I said to her, "I know what you are going through, my ex-husband has not given me anything for our children for over three years and it is so hard."

Let me back up here a little. When he decided he would tell her I was his cousin, I didn't think of it then, but now I do. This cousin bit seems to be a good story for him because now that I am writing this, I remember a few months after our marriage he brought a girl home whom he introduced to me as his cousin. It was not until months later, when his mother was visiting, I told her, "Oh, by the way, so and so was here," I don't remember her name. She then asked, who? I repeated myself, "So and so, you know, your son's cousin came to visit few days ago."

She, may she rest in peace, said he had no cousin with that name.

So...back to where I left off. I was introduced to his wife as his cousin. Things were fine until this particular night when she was pouring her heart out in the kitchen and I sympathized with her. At this point, he, not wanting to be the big bad wolf about not supporting his children, shouted at me. "What do you mean, I am not supporting the children, didn't I send you money some time ago?" When he realized what he had said, he covered his mouth in shock and looked at her. She said very quietly (she is a very quiet and soft spoken person), "It's all right. I knew she was your ex-wife all along."

I said "How did you know?"

She said, "I saw your pictures."

I turned to him and said, "What money have you sent us? You have not sent any money for over three years." This blew up into a heated argument because apparently he was telling her that he was sending his children money every month; so naturally, she wanted to know what had happened to the money he claimed he was sending. He turned to me and told me to get out of his house immediately because I had come to America to break up his home. Of course I knew no one and had nowhere to stay, so he called his sister, may she rest in peace, and asked her to take me in. She gave me directions on the phone and I left.

When I opened the door to leave, I saw snow on the ground so high that I did not know what to do. That morning was the first time I had ever seen snow. He had called me to the window to show me what snow looked like, but it looked so flimsy falling down that when I saw the pile on the ground, I could not believe that those tiny flakes could have piled so high. It was falling all day. I had no choice but to walk in it—with my high heels and cotton Jamaican dress. Thank God, the day after I arrived at his house, he asked me, "You landed in New York, in March, without a coat?" Of course I had no coat. What did I know about coats in Jamaica? He had taken me to buy a spring coat. I later learned that there were spring coats and winter coats. Needless to say, I fell several times before reaching the subway station. At one stage when I fell, my suitcase opened, but I was so cold, I could not stop to gather my things properly, so I scraped garbage and whatever into it.

I thought walking in the snow was bad but more was to come. When I reached the station and looked up, I realized I had to walk up thirty-five steps to the train. I could not believe it. I was so tired from the walk; I knew I would not make it up the stairs. I started to cry. I counted every stair I stepped on to reach the top, and every step I took, all thirty-five of them, I cursed my ex with tears in my eyes. This was my first subway ride. What a ride it was, rolling and shaking.

My sister-in-law sent her younger sister, who knew me, and her husband to meet me. At that time, I had never met him.

As soon as my sister-in-law saw me, she got busy. She started rubbing my body with a very strong Jamaican White Rum. She and her husband worked on my feet with hot towels and wrapped me in warm clothes because I was almost freezing.

The very next day on her way to work, she took me to an agency. I was placed in a job that same day at 444 Fifth Avenue, New York, as secretary to their import manager. That weekend my sister-in-law found a room for me in a rooming house in Brooklyn where her cousin was living.

Working and Living in New York

Coming from a small country like Jamaica to a huge city like New York was, of course, shocking. Paper would not be enough to write about all the experiences I went through in New York. I would be lost for hours trying to find my way home. I would take the Uptown train when I should be on the Downtown train and vice versa. I would fall in the snow repeatedly. I would have to hold on to trees, cars, anything to steady my walk in the snow with those heels. More was to come!

The first day going to work, before going underground to take the train, I used the pizza shop at the corner of the street as a mark, so I would have no problem finding my way home in the evening. Was I in for a major surprise! When I arrived at the station that evening and went upstairs to the street, I did not see one pizza shop, instead there were four pizza shops, one at every corner. I cried. I had no idea where to turn. It had taken me hours to find my train and hours to find my way home with everyone giving me different directions. I hated big, big, big, New York.

I wanted to go back to Jamaica so badly, but I had no money for my ticket. I wrote my mother letter after letter to explain my situation but could not mail them because I did not have the money to purchase stamps.

I wanted to send money to my children so badly but had none. Thank God for my mother and my first paycheck.

Because I could now afford stamps, I wrote not only to my mother but to close friends who I knew were concerned about my well being. One of them was the late Angie, may she rest in peace.

Help in the Midst of My Storm

Angie was so sorry for me that she sent me her mother's name and address in Brooklyn.

She told me to go and look her up. I did. The minute I walked into her cozy apartment, I felt at home. She told me to leave where I was and come to live with her. I jumped at the opportunity and moved in.

She became my mother away from my mother. She gave me a home away from home. We did things together. She helped me in so many ways that at this point God knows them all and he will bless, and has blessed, her.

Thunderbolt in My Storm

About a year later, one Monday morning the comptroller of the firm called me. When I went inside his office, two men from the immigration department were there to greet me. I was working as a secretary and, you guessed it, someone reported to the Immigration department that I had no papers to work in America. They gave me a few days to leave the country. I was to take my passport to them the next day. I was so nervous and afraid I did not know what to do. I wanted with all my heart to return to Jamaica, but I did not want to go back penniless. I wanted to look back on my hassle in America and say, "At least I achieved something." At this point, I had nothing as I was just working day to day for survival.

Candy to the Rescue

I was riding the subway home that evening, deep in thought. I looked up and saw a young lady on the train. She looked just like my schoolmate and girlfriend from Jamaica, but I knew it was not her because she was studying and living in London. I also knew that she had a sister in America, so I thought this must be her. I just kept staring at her but I said nothing. Finally, when I got off the train to go home, to my surprise, she got off also. I still said nothing. Then I realized she was behind me, and she was walking in the same direction I was going. I could not believe it. After a while, I decided to turn around and say something to her. I said, "Are you Candy, and you have a sister in London?"

She said yes. I almost flipped. I was in America almost one year. She was living around the corner from me and I did not know this?

She had visited Jamaica when I was in commercial school. Her sister had already left our commercial school to continue her studies in London, so their other sister asked if I could show her around the island. I did and enjoyed every minute. She was a real neat, sophisticated, educated person. I instantly became one of her admirers. You know, teenagers always have an idol. After we got over the excitement of meeting each other again, we talked about everything. Eventually, I told her I wished we had met sooner because I now had to start preparing to return to Jamaica. She asked why. I told her the Immigration department came to my office today and told me to bring my passport to them tomorrow. I told her the entire story while we stood on Park Place.

Rescued from My Storm

She told me not to turn in my passport to them because they were going to deport me immediately. I was shocked. She gave me her address and told me to meet her tomorrow. The next day, she introduced me to her sister-in-law who later played a great role in my life. She was a business woman in Brooklyn, a member of various professional organizations, including the Professional Black Business Women of Brooklyn. As time passed, she became instrumental in my life. She got me involved in the modeling world, at first with hairdos, then hands, shoes, and finally clothes. I had previously modeled coats with the import company where I worked on Park Avenue before the Immigration department stepped in.

Rising Above the Storms

This woman not only knew the right people in the right places, she went to the right places. She was a go-getter. I soon learned the ropes of survival in the Big City.

She made an appointment for me to register with a domestic agency to apply for a live-in job. I told everyone, including my sister-in-law, that I was returning to Jamaica. I shipped all my office clothes to my sister in Jamaica as I would no longer be using them, and entered a home as a domestic maid. I did not want to, but I had no choice. I did not want to return to Jamaica empty handed and broke. The first day I put my maid uniform on, I could not believe it. I wanted to leave immediately, but I had to focus. I had a goal. That part was not so bad; I *truly* broke down when I started to wash the kitchen floor on my knees that night. This woman had a white wooden kitchen floor. Dinner had to be cooked every night - the entire course; you had to serve dinner in the formal dining room and dessert in the family room. The works! Because of the daily traffic on this white wooden kitchen floor, the floor had to be washed every night. I vividly remember washing the floor that first night. As I was on my knees washing it, I started to cry. My tears were running with the cleaning water. I felt so degraded, that I decided the first pay check would be my ticket home. That night I sat down and wrote a letter to my mother to keep her abreast of my life and tell her about my situation.

My mother, as I have said before, was not educated because she was left an orphan at an early age. She was not educated *book-wise* but she sure was educated *life-wise*. Mama gave us such good advice that even now I look back sometimes and wonder how on earth did she ever know what she knew with her limited education.

Mama wrote me back. I will never forget some of the words in that letter as long as I live, which I will repeat here. I have repeated them over and over again to people. She said, "Never you cry over anything you do for an honest living because what you have in your head, no man can take it out."

Brothers and sisters, those words resounded in my head. They were my inspiration for the duration of my stay in America, and as a matter of fact, from that day I decided I would work at any job I got because I was a legal and executive secretary, therefore, one day, I would go back to my secretarial job.

Facing My Storms Head On

I worked hard as a maid, a nurse, a babysitter, chambermaid, you name it, in order to save and go home. I remember the first live-in nurse job I got. This gentleman had to get an injection every day. The money was great, so I told his daughter I could work with him. But when I heard about the injection part of it I got scared, so I told the agency that I was not really a nurse and I had no idea how to give an injection. The woman at the agency called the nurse at the doctor's office and told her. The nurse asked me to come over to her office—she gave me an orange and a needle, she made me practice and practice until she felt I was capable of giving this gentleman an injection. I did and he never knew the difference. I kept those needles for years as a reminder that I could do anything if I had to. That job was temporary and ended upon arrival of his daughter. I was able to save quite a lot of money from that one.

I should add that with these jobs, you were entitled to one day off per week. It was called "Alice's Day Off." It took me a while to figure out who "Alice" was. I would take the train from the islands to Brooklyn to visit with friends but would return more tired than I had left because of the distance. I thought that was a waste of time, so from 1964 to 1966 I decided to use my day off to go to school. I entered John Robert Powers Modeling School for their morning and afternoon classes and Stenotype Academy on Broadway for their evening classes, where I studied Court Reporting.

My other job was a nursemaid and nanny with a prominent artist and his family. They were a beautiful young couple with a precious baby boy. My job was to take care of this precious baby. During the course of working with them, I decided to return to Jamaica, but before doing so I asked them if they could sponsor my mother to the States. I figured since my mother was looking after my children for almost two years in Jamaica, she had gotten so attached to them, if I went home and just took them away from her she would be devastated. It would break her heart. So the best thing I could do was to have her come to America. That would be a sweet transition for her and I could return to Jamaica to take care of my children.

This couple willingly sponsored my mother into the United States. My mother would take my place caring for their child, since I was leaving the States. My mother came to the States and took my job.

I went to work for a gorgeous single mother, taking care of her two wonderful children. Another beautiful family. In fact, working for this family was the best.

However, in the midst of preparing to return to Jamaica I realized that Mama would be alone in America after I left. I could not leave her alone. Years ago, Mama had sent my eldest sister to complete her studies in England, but as most Jamaicans who were sent overseas to study, she never returned to Jamaica. I remembered that my sister always wanted to go to America because she would be paid more. I thought, if I was able to get her here also, she could be with Mama.

Now, this young woman I was working with worked at the Capital Building in Albany. I decided to ask her if she would sponsor my sister, Fay, now deceased. She agreed but I had to work another year with her pending the entry of my sister into the States. I did.

No one in our family had seen Fay for over ten years. Mama had sold a piece of property and used the funds to send her to England to study. After her studies, she worked and lived in London as a registered nurse in medical surgical nursing. Later she married and had two children. Although this was going to be a great reunion, I did not stick around for her arrival because three weeks before she came to America, I left for Jamaica. I planned it that way because I did not want another day of winter. Daily I was glued to the TV to hear news of the weather. I listened intensely just to know when it was going to snow. I would rush and pack as fast as I could, trying to beat the snow, even though I would not be able to see my sister.

It was then more than two years that I had been 'in hiding' from the Immigration department. As soon as I purchased my ticket, shipped and packed my belongings, I called and told them I was returning to Jamaica. To my amazement they had an officer at the airport waiting for me to ensure that I was leaving.

Thank God, I was then twenty-six years old; I had all I needed, I was returning to my children. I stood inside the plane, looked back at America and said, *"God truly Bless America."* *That's* how I wanted to leave America, *that's* how I left America. America gave me a start in life and I ran with it.

My Return to Jamaica

Starting Life All Over Again

I returned to Jamaica and, of course, I had to get to know my children all over again. By this time they did not remember me. They were one, two, and three when I left Jamaica to get a start in life. I did not return wealthy where money was concerned, but I returned wealthy in wisdom, experience, how to live, and be prepared for life.

I learnt that in America you are just another number, another person, so since no one knew you, you could do all sorts of jobs without feeling embarrassed.

In Jamaica, however, that was not the case. Menial jobs, or at least what people called "menial jobs," would have been a no-no for me.

After settling my children in schools, I got a job the very week I arrived, through Manpower Agency. I was brave now, so a little later, I decided it was time for me to get an additional job as I needed more income.

I wanted to work nights. The only night job I wanted was that of a hostess. I wanted something happy and fun. I could not work as a secretary day and night; it would have been too stressful.

Before leaving Jamaica, I would never, ever have thought of working as an hostess. That would have been below my dignity. However, because I was exposed in New York, working any job, not looking down on them, I now had an open mind.

I figured, if I could wash off my makeup, put on a chambermaid uniform, put on a maid uniform, work as a housekeeper, nanny, dog walker, etc. (same woman), then I could also put my makeup on, put sexy clothes on, and work as an hostess or waitress (same woman). I was told that I could make money in this job, but I had no idea how much money until I jumped in and made the plunge.

I decided if I was going to work two jobs, I was going to purchase a house. I did not have one cent towards this, but I could work two jobs and pay for a house. I did instead of paying rent.

Creating and Making a Home for My Children and I

I had friends in high places in Jamaica because, as I mentioned before, you are somebody in Jamaica, not just a number.

One day I went to the bank to see a friend of mine who was the bank manager. I asked him for a loan of $1,000 as a down payment on a house. In 1970, $1,000 to me was a lot of money. I explained to him that I had seen an ad in the newspaper where they were building middle income homes in a new development named Independence City. The required deposit was $1,000. The monthly mortgage was $64. I was paying monthly rent of $68; hence, I could afford to pay the mortgage and own instead of renting, especially since I had three children for whom to provide a home.

He asked me how I intended to pay back the loan and the mortgage at the same time. I told him I was going to get a night job, live off that job, then deposit my weekly salary from my day job into his bank to cover his loan. It took quite a while with more and more discussions in his office, but he finally said to me, "I am going to lend you this $1,000.00 but don't let me down." I promised him I would not. I got the loan, left the bank, went directly to the developers, made the down payment on my little house.

Purchasing My First House

A three-bedroom, two-bathroom house in Independence City. The purchase price for this house was $7,444. I lived in this house with my children, making it into a lovely home for us. It was not much, but it was home. I worked two jobs for two years and eleven months. During this time, I met so many men, lived such a hectic and fast life, space would not permit everything. However, I will briefly describe my life as a hostess/waitress and as a secretary at the same time.

Secretary by Day, Hostess by Night

Needless to say, the two jobs were as different as day is from night. I was basically a sweet, unspoilt young woman who just wanted to get as much out of life as she could for herself and her three children. I worked as a secretary on Duke Street from 8:00 a.m. to 4:00 p.m. and as a hostess and waitress from 5:00 p.m. to 2:00 a.m. As I mentioned before, if I had not lived in New York, my mind would not have been "wide" enough to let me accept an hostess/waitress job.

In any event, since most Jamaicans still had very "narrow minds," of course, they did not accept my hostess/waitress job. It did not bother me, as a matter of fact, it became a joke to me after a while, because I was beginning to learn a lot about our "corporate workplace workers."

I would be in the lounge of the hotel at nights doing my hostess and waitress job. I would see secretaries from Duke Street coming in with their dates. They would ignore me and pretend they did not see me. The very next day, I would be on Duke Street going to lunch or having lunch. I would see those same girls who ignored me the night before, waving and smiling at me. Pretty soon I realized what was happening, so I turned the tide.

I just completely ignored them, day and night. I completely looked beyond them as if they were non-existent and went about my business.

Their being hypocritical was bad, but worse was to come. As the weeks went on into months at my night job, it turned out that I had the last laugh. You see, at Happy Hour each day, the men who walked in with them had just taken home another girl or his wife, whom he was with earlier. Now, he was walking in with them. They never knew this. They apparently thought they were his one and only date for the evening. Pretty soon, or sometimes even after midnight, the men would take the second set of women home and walk in with yet another woman. Our staff would have such a laugh at these girls because they flaunted being in this plush hotel with their nose in the air so much, not knowing they were just being used by these men. It would have been funny, if it wasn't so sad. I may have looked small in their eyes but they looked even smaller in mine.

Not to mention, most of these men, especially the playboy types who would visit our lounge, talked about everything they did, had done, or were going to do with these women. I listened a lot, laughed a little, and learned a lot just by just being with them.

Then and there, in this lounge, I decided, "Forget these men, there is no way I would ever be going with any of them, so they could take my name all over Jamaica."

After working at the hotel for over a year, my social life was nothing because I was basically tired after working two jobs anyway. I did nothing but work, and work, and go home. I had no time for men.

One night, this gorgeous blue-eyed, tall, knock-out good looking blond man was sitting by himself. He was in my station. After I had waited on him, he started a conversation with me. We always talked to the customers, but I could not get rid of this one. When he had to leave, he lingered and lingered. He then came over to our corner, the hostesses' "private" corner, to talk to us. He eventually asked me for a dinner date. I told him I could not because I worked two jobs and would not be able to find the time. He insisted. He asked me if I never got a night off. I said yes but that was the night I stayed home with my children, gave the maid a night off, and rested. He said he would pay another maid for the night to stay with the children. I told him it was not the payment of another maid, it was just being with my children. I went to serve others but he never left our corner. He insisted. I had to get rid of him. The other hostesses told me to expect these "dates" and the only way to get rid of him, since he was not leaving, was to go out with him, because he would only come back tomorrow, and tomorrow, etc. Finally, I said okay.

Thursday night was my night off. Independence City was very far from the hotel. I told him he could talk to any of the taxi drivers at the hotel, to bring him to my home; they all knew where each hostess lived, as from time to time they have to take us home. Thursday night, it was not one of the taxis from the hotel that pulled up at my gate. Instead it was a limo. I figured whoever gave him my address, knew he was coming to get me, so it was safe.

He took me to the Blue Mountain Inn. This was the first time since my return to Jamaica that I had gone to the Blue Mountain Inn, one of the finest, most exquisite restaurants in Jamaica. He was a dream. We had a wonderful evening. The best wine, the best food, the best company, he treated me like royalty. By the end of the evening we had warmed up to each other and I was ready to go all the way with him. Such a beautiful night, I enjoyed his company and attention. We did go all the way. The next morning while making my bed, there was $200 under under my pillow. I was in shock.

My Social Life

Gosh…As the weeks went by… I thought to myself, *I had/have no social life…I just work and work. Maybe…just maybe…* I was thinking…*These foreign men are charming, handsome, classy, white business men. They treat you with respect and class. They take you to the best places. They open car doors for you. They pour your wine. They pull your chairs. They are intelligent, you can talk with them for hours. They just give you money after they treat you to a blissful night, without even asking whether or not you need it, while not even my ex gives me a dollar for his children?* I kept thinking…

I started comparing them with local men. Then and there, I decided from then on, I would date only foreign men. Well, that first night was the beginning of many more evenings with other expatriates and foreigners. Some would be leaving the next day or the same night, so I knew that my business was safe. As a matter of fact, I thought no one would ever know; I could live independently and provide for myself and my children. *Hello?*

Even then sometimes I would still run short of money since I had the mortgage, light, water, groceries, school fees, lunch money, maid, gardener, you name it, and myself to take care of. It was no easy joke to provide for three children by yourself in Jamaica. Jamaica is so hard that people call it "the Rock."

I used to say, "No one will know," but of course now I know that *someone* did know; He knew all the time. That *someone* not only knew but he saw. Also, I kept insisting that I had to provide for my children. I had no idea that I had a *Provider*. I worked for years, night and day in Kingston, until I changed jobs and relocated to Ocho Rios on the North Coast.

This was a big change for us; the children moved school and went to Iona Boarding School. They adjusted well in the beginning and so did I. However, the situation where I worked became very sticky, one in which I did not want to partake. So on the advice of several people I looked for employment elsewhere. I did not want to return to Kingston immediately and take the children from School, so I took a job in Runaway Bay closer to Ocho Rios where they went to school.

One night while sitting at the bar in the hotel I saw a young man pass by. I thought he looked familiar, but I said nothing. Soon thereafter a friend came in who lived in Kingston. We were glad to see each other and while we chatted, the young man came up to her and she introduced us. I then realized that I did know him. Not only did I know him, we grew up together as children. Now he was a grown man and he was gay.

Just when you thought you knew it all, or you had seen it all, something new popped up. This was the first time in my life I was going to actually know a person who was gay. I knew people were that way by just looking at them, but it never affected me because I never knew them. They were not my friends. However, because this guy and I grew up together, I relaxed with him and his friend as the evening went on. After we closed the hotel that night we all headed down the road to a nightclub. This was my first night out in Runaway Bay and they made it a great one for me. We danced, we laughed, we had so much fun. The best part of the evening to me was that after we all had so much fun we just parted as friends. At this stage of my life, having these gay guys as friends was great for me because I was at the stage of my life where I was fed up with the men scene.

My children were teenagers now; I had more or less a comfortable foundation. I had left the hotel business for years. I had settled down with a wonderful Jamaican man, eight years younger than I. Later we broke up because I felt he needed to have children and a life and home for himself, which I was not prepared to give him. I had not gone out with men for years. Now, I did not need them or their money. I just wanted to go dancing with them, have a good time, have clean fun, and go home. So when these gay men came into my life they came at the right time.

By the next day I was thinking, "This is great. I have two guys to go out with and no bed involved, wonderful!" We became a trio in Runaway Bay. I was good for them, and they were good for me. I was good for them because they had a woman between them, and they were good for me because I had men to shelter me.

However, as with everything else in life, one never sees down the road. I had no idea how far this would have gone. I soon returned to Kingston. We kept in touch with each other.

I did not go back to the hotel business. Neither did I know that the hotel business was a little Peyton Place, where everybody knew everybody. Whenever they visited me in Kingston, it was for us to do the town. They took me to another hotel in Kingston. There I would meet another gay friend of theirs. Pretty soon I would go to house parties with them, most of the time I would be the only woman there, still having fun with them because I did not want to lose their friendship and lose my "social times."

Before I knew it, I had met over a hundred gay men. I had no idea there were so many gay men in Jamaica, and most of them were in high places.

This went on for a long time and then one of the gang decided to take me and my girlfriend, who had just returned to Jamaica after traveling for a while, to a club he had just opened. He did not tell us what kind of club it was, and we never guessed, but maybe you are smarter than we were at that time, so you have already guessed it. It was a gay club. I never dreamt of a gay club in Jamaica. At first, I thought this was one big joke.

I remember vividly saying to myself when we sat down, "Oh God have mercy on *them*." You see, *they* needed prayer.

I didn't. *Big joke.* I really was hurting inside watching them because I had never seen men dancing together until that night in a club. I knew this was going too far, but I kept going out with them.

Moving on Up

I decided that I had outgrown the area of Independence City. I wanted to move up in life. I wanted to live in the better part of town, closer to my friends. I kept thinking about it but not planning. It so happened that one day I went home from work and someone had broken into my house. I was so afraid that my final decision was made immediately to sell the house.

In 1970, I had deposited one thousand dollars on my first house. The purchase price was $7,444.

I lived in it for five years.

In 1975, I put it on the market for sale.

It was sold for twenty-three thousand dollars cash. I did not go through any bank or mortgage company, the buyer was coming home directly from London to retire. He had the cash. He purchased my house.

Around this time, my friends were leaving Jamaica. They told me to take the money out of Jamaica and deposit it on a house in Miami. I had no intention of leaving Jamaica. I told them I could not live in Miami on the same level that I lived in Jamaica; I would just be another number. I was comparing moving to Miami with my experiences of living in New York during my younger years. They apparently knew more about what was going to happen in Jamaica, than I did because I was never interested in politics. I only liked one politician because of the great things he did for downtown Kingston. Before I met him, I was amazed to see the clean city when I returned to Jamaica. I commended him not knowing that later I would have had the privilege of working for and with him. Sometimes I did not listen to the news, or even bother to vote. If I had the time I would, if I did not have the time, I would not.

Purchasing My Second house, My Dream Home

After I paid off the balance of the mortgage on the house, paid off all my bills, I still had fifteen thousand dollars. I used this as a deposit on my dream house, in my dream area, New Kingston. I worked hard on this place. I spent four thousand dollars for carpeting. It was a beautiful three-story townhouse; my bedroom was on the third floor. Each floor had a bathroom and a terrace. The terrace on the third floor was converted into a fourth bedroom. My son occupied that bedroom. The two bedrooms on the second floor I rented out. My mortgage was $215 per month. The rent coming in from the two rooms was $300 per month.

These rooms were rented out because by this time my daughter had gone to New York to visit with my mother, and she decided that she loved America and wanted to stay. My older son had gone to California to be with his father, who had turned up in Jamaica after many years and decided that he wanted to help the children by taking them to live with him in California, which did not work out. Within three months they were back in Jamaica cursing him. They were afraid of him. However, a few more years had passed since then; they were now older, so when he asked that they come again, only my oldest son wanted to go. There would be more opportunities for him there, so I sent him.

My youngest child, Christopher, was with me in Jamaica. He was attending Calabar College. He insisted that he did not want to leave Jamaica.

Since the rent coming in could cover my mortgage, I was more financially stable, so I decided I would semi-retire. I would keep my job at the hotel and work Mondays, Wednesdays, and Fridays. I planned all this and targeted for it.

New Storms a Coming

Just as soon as I decided life was stable and I could semi-retire, here we went again with winds of hurricane force. Politics took a wild turn in Jamaica. The government started talking about socialism and America's democratic lifestyle. They were saying things like, if we Jamaicans did not like it, there were five flights per day to Miami and we could leave. People took those flights. But not I. Things got worse. Jamaicans were killing each other like idiots.

Things were going from bad to worse. I then noticed that Americans, Canadians, English, Australians, along with their companies, were closing and leaving Jamaica. I figured if they were smarter than I was, and they were leaving so fast, something must be going on that I did not know about, so I got more interested in politics.

I soon learned that socialism was the avenue the country was taking. I decided to emigrate—but too late. American dollars were nowhere to be found. By this time, Jamaicans could not take more than fifty US dollars out of the country. My son still insisted that he did not want to leave.

Since there was no foreign currency in the banks, one of my friends loaned me US$12.

I decided to leave Jamaica with that twelve US dollars. It was agreed that the rooms would still be rented out. My son would occupy the top floor using the rent for survival and I would pay the mortgage from Miami. Miami had its *storms* but thank God they led me to my savior, the Lord Jesus Christ.

Victories in My Life

The Villages, FL 32163

Although I became a member of St. Louis Catholic Church, I still kept in touch with my friends at the Baptist Church.

I am very happy to state here and now that almost all my friends from the Baptist church visited St. Louis while I was there and they all loved it. I had met a very gentle divorced man in the singles group when I attended the Baptist church. He was once a Catholic but left the faith and became a Baptist. He was married to a very sweet, beautiful woman. She was also a Baptist. They went through rough times and divorced.

One day, years later, his wife called me to say that she was praying this morning while taking her walk, when the Lord told her to call me and ask me to give her husband a message for her.

After this intervention, the Lord used me to take the man's wife to St. Louis. He started coming also. His mother, a devoted Catholic who lived in a different state, would attend St. Louis with them whenever she visited Miami. She would share with me how very happy she was that her son had come back to the church. Later, his wife went through the RCIA program and became a Catholic. God truly worked in their lives because they were remarried here at St. Louis Catholic Church. At their wedding, most of the guests were from, you guessed it, the Baptist church where we all attended.

I outlined the above, which is only one of the many victorious events in which the Lord used me as an instrument for his kingdom, while on my exciting journey with him. Praise his holy name!

Mary, Mother of God

Back then, many people, especially my Baptist and non-Catholic friends, who would sometimes question me about my Catholic church, asked me if I prayed to Mary. I would always say, "No, but I ask her to pray for me."

I would also hear numerous complaints from well meaning beautiful Catholics in St. Louis, like myself, about the deep devotion given by some in our church to Mary, which at times to us seemed to take priority over Jesus Christ, our Lord and Savior.

Even though I made this determination in my mind, I would tell them, "Don't knock the people who say the rosary, Mary will always point them to Jesus because she says, 'Do whatever he tells you.' Hence, I will not knock them, but I won't say the rosary."

I have always said and insisted that I will never say the rosary. God himself will have to make me say the rosary.

I have heard many beautiful teachings on the rosary. The first one was at a past Catholic Charismatic Conference.

Soon thereafter, one night at our prayer meeting, dear departed Fred came up to me and handed me a little circular rosary. I am sure Fred, like many others, thought that since I was so involved in the church, I was saying the rosary.

I took it and put it in a drawer at home. Weeks after this, "How to Say the Rosary" was pictured and printed in our church bulletin. It seemed as if I was all of a sudden being bombarded with the rosary. I had thrown out several Bulletins since the one with the printed rosary information, but for some reason I kept this one. I just said to myself these are nice writings and things, but not for me. God himself will have to tell me to say the rosary.

Four months passed. The very last time I said this was on Sunday, December 7, 1985, at the Dade County Stockade in Miami, where I told a prisoner that my friend, who gave him the rosary, prays the rosary, but I don't and God himself will have to let me know differently. This friend of mine had helped me take prisoners to church this one particular Sunday. At the prison center, she had gone around giving all the prisoners a rosary. I was furious with her for doing this because I told her they did not even know the meaning of these rosaries. They were only wearing them around their necks as necklaces. I told her this while we were going home from the prison.

God Still Speaks

Tuesday, December 9, 1985, with no thought of anything on my mind I went to bed. During my sleep I dreamt or had a vision which went like this:

> The sky became pitch black as if it was midnight. A glow fell over part of the sky like rays of yellow/gold.

It looked as if the sky met the Earth and everything was one flaming ball. I said to myself, looks like the end of the world. I then looked over to one corner of the sky and I saw the head of a woman, I knew she was a saint because of the halo around her head. To me she was not the Virgin Mary I knew because I had never seen her before. I stared at her in awe. The size of her head became so big that it filled half of the sky. She had a tear in one eye. The tear was not running, so I knew she was not moving as a person, she was just a picture planted in the sky.

I turned to my mother who was standing beside me in my dream and said, "Mama look, look," and we turned around to look. This time, I saw her rising to heaven, then the Virgin Mary with whom I was familiar, appeared beneath her. Both pictures slowly ascended into heaven. I fell to my knees and said to my mother, "My God, Mama, do you see this?" I turned around but my mother was not there. Instead I was looking at a Jamaican Oriental woman who was our Religious Ed teacher at church. I jumped out of my sleep, shaking.

In the morning when I got out of bed, I kept talking to the Lord, asking him what was the meaning of my dream. I said, "Lord, you said in your Word that we should not make unto ourselves any graven thing." I stopped. I repeated the word, *thing* over and over again. I heard myself saying, Mary is not a *thing*. She is a person. She is the mother of God. I ran for my Bible. I looked carefully at the wording. It said *thing*. I looked at my other Bible. It said *thing*. I looked up the complete meaning of the word *thing* in the dictionary. The word *thing* did not describe a person. This was a very stunning revelation to me. All this happened on the night of Tuesday, December 9, 1985.

I called our Religious Ed Teacher first thing the next morning, Wednesday, December 10, 1985 telling her of my dream or vision.

While I was telling her, my mother was awake, lying beside me in bed. After I hung up, my mother turned to me and said, "Are you crazy, how could you be a Catholic and don't say the rosary?" My mother said the rosary daily. I got dressed and left for work. Instead of our usual Thursday night prayer meeting at church, a healing Mass was to take place in our main church that night, Thursday, December 11, 1985.

I had no idea who the visiting priest was who would be doing the Mass. Before I left home, I told my mother that if he was boring, I would be leaving. Therefore, when she saw me rise in the church to leave she should also get up to leave with me. I told my mother before, because she had difficulties hearing and I did not want her to shout, "Are we leaving ?" to interrupt the Mass. She said okay.

Just before the Mass, not knowing what to expect, a very devoted couple in the church came into the sanctuary, heading for the altar. The wife had some sort of book in her hand. They faced the altar with their backs to the congregation they bowed, she placed it on the altar, bowed again, and left.

As they were leaving, I almost fainted. They had placed a picture of the Virgin Mary, the second one I saw in my dream, on the altar, only her face was turned in the opposite direction.

I did not think my mother could see so far, but she started to tremble and said, "Your dream, your dream, did

God ever tell you anything about me? Your dream, your dream." I had to calm her down. I said, "Mama, I need to listen and hear what is going on."

The Mass started. A young woman, who came in with the priest, took the mike and began explaining or narrating a beautiful story of the Blessed Mother who had appeared to this Mexican in Mexico. She was Our Lady of Guadalupe. My mother started to shake, she said to me, "My God this is your dream, if you had not told me before, I would never believe you after hearing this." I said, "I know." I said, "Lord, Thank you for talking to me so plainly."

On my way home, I started to think real hard where I had seen the other saint or Mary with the tear in her eye. Then I remembered it was my friend who gave out the books and rosaries at the prison. I remember that I did not like the look of the saint on the book at all. I also remembered that she was black.

I knew I had to find out more about her, so the following Sunday, when I saw her at church I asked her if she had another book. Sure enough she did. I did not even think as to whether or not it was her last book, I just asked her for it. She gave it to me. Monday morning I looked through the book for some information on this black saint but could find nothing. There was an address and phone number on the back of the book, so I called the office in Michigan. Someone promised to send me literatures on the saint. I said thank God, that is that, now I can rest this case.

Needless to say, literature, including two books came. The Mary I saw in my dream was Our Lady of Czestochowa (pronounced Chan sto ho va), frequently called the Black Madonna, because this Mary and her infant son were of deep bronze color. I believe because I am black, the Lord made a Black Madonna appear to me.

The literature explained that Poland was going through a religious crisis. You could count on your fingers, the poor remnants of Catholic schools. Hundreds of Catholic kindergartens were closed. Sisters were removed from hospitals. During this crisis, the Polish people had recourse to the Blessed Virgin, under her title, and at the shrine of Our Lady of Czestochowa, located atop Jasna Gora (the Bright Mountain) in a Monastery Church of the Order of St. Paul the Hermit. The shrine dates from the fourteenth century.

The monastery was established as an act of thanksgiving, by King Wladyslaw, after he had effected the conversion of Lithuania to the true Faith. The painting is enshrined there and was brought to Jasna Gora soon after the founding of the monastery. Legend has it that the Black Madonna was painted by St. Luke the Evangelist on the top of a table built by St. Joseph for use in the Holy Family's Nazareth home. It remained there until Our Lady's Assumption.

The tear I saw running down her face was not a tear. It was a scar. This scar was inflicted with a sword. Robbers had looted the shrine and were rushing from the town when their horses stopped short and could not be prodded into moving. One of the thieves, sure that the theft of the painting accounted for the animals' obstinacy, hurled it from the cart. (A spring, over which a chapel has been built, is said to have erupted at the spot where it struck the ground). It split, and another of the robbers, angered because it had slowed their escape, marred it with his sword. He was struck dead. His frightened companions fled. The townspeople returned the damaged painting to the shrine.

Wednesday, December 16, 1985, as I was preparing to have my morning devotions I looked at my altar in my home and said, "I must get a statue of the Virgin Mary and a glass rosary to keep on my altar."

I went to work. Later that day, I received a call from a friend at church, a sociologist in the prisons. She said, "Elnieda, Sunday I saw your mother saying the rosary in church and I commented to myself, *Strange, I have never seen Elnieda saying the rosary*, however, she dismissed it. That morning she realized that every two weeks she took the statue of our Lady of Fatima to individual homes for two weeks. This was the day it would be returned to her to be passed on to someone else. She continued, "This morning I prayed, 'Okay, Blessed Mother, who do you want me to put you with this time?'" She said Elnieda immediately came to her mind, so she calling me, very excitedly to ask if I wanted her.

I said, "Yes and did you hear of my vision?"

She said, "No, what vision?"

I said "You really did not hear of it and that is why you decided to send her to me?"

She said "No."

I said, "Alright, just sit tight and I will tell it to you tonight at our EE classes."

She said, "Okay."

Then I said to her, "I will have to purchase a rosary, though."

She said, "Don't, Elnieda; I will give you one tonight."

Is our God real? Does he still speak to us? Does he answer prayers? Even the dumb ones we shout out at him? *Yes he does, praise his holy name!*

I have prayed the rosary ever since that day.

Terry came into my life

September 23, 2013

Dear Readers:

I met Elnieda (Ellie) Sinclair while attending a Why Catholic group in her home. Our small group formed very close friendships and helped each other in our spiritual journey.

We enjoyed each other's company and guidance so much that we decided to continue our weekly meetings to further discuss and read other books about leading a Christian Life.

Ellie was always the rock behind our group. We all enjoyed listening to her recount stories about her past and could not wait for our next meeting to hear more. She is a very cultured, intelligent individual with extensive knowledge.

Her book, Get Up, Stand Up & Rise - the Best is Yet To Come, will be a moving and inspirational piece of literature. I think this book will captivate the readers so well that once they read this book they will feel that they also know Ellie like I do and look forward to the next chapter.

Wishing her the best

Mrs. Terry M. Hudgens

Immaculate Heart of Mary, Ocala, Florida

In December 2007, I retired and moved to Ocala, Florida.

In 2008, I became a member of The Cenacle Prayer Group at Immaculate Heart of Mary Catholic Church, in Ocala, Florida.

Does God have a sense of humor? A member of a church with Mother Mary's name!

Please note:

> The purpose of my writing these little stories is not to convince anyone to do what I do—but to share with you the things God has revealed to me, and done through me. To let you know that God will reveal to any of us anything we ask of him. All we have to do is ask and seek him with all our hearts.

The Bible

I grew up like the average child, going to church on Sundays, but believing that God was way up in the heavens where He lived, that we should do good, or else. That's called the fear of God (in the mind of a child).

I also knew there was a Bible. This Bible contained laws and rules we should live by.

This Bible contained stories about saints, prophets, and great kings.

Beautiful and sad things happened to them but to me that was a long, long, time ago. We were now living in modern days.

After I became born-again in 1979 I started reading the Bible. I only knew the King James version of the Bible with its beautiful old English. I would go from church to church and hear other people read from their Bibles. They also sounded beautiful. Some sounded more beautiful than mine. I quickly learned that they all meant the same thing, that the words were only more modern. I loved theirs, but I decided to stick with the King James Version because it was a challenge for me.

A challenge in that before I was born-again I never understood many things in the Bible. It was just a nice book with rhymes and poetries. What I soon discovered was that even though I had the old version of the King James in my hand, when others would read from their modern Bible, I would know the modern English before they even finished reading. This became very exciting to me. Later I also learned that the Holy Spirit was the person who reveals, teaches the scriptures to us. That he revealed scriptures to individuals. I remember thinking once. "Man, I am truly understanding the Bible, how come? I could not understand why until I realized that the blessed Holy Spirit, who is always with us, where two or three are gathered in his name, while we read his Word, teaches and guides us, once we acknowledge and welcome his presence. One night my bubbles were about to burst. This happened about four years after I was born-again.

Incidentally, I was born-again at home. Soon thereafter I made my profession of faith in a Baptist church where I was a member for two years. (That's another story.) However, my spiritual bubbles were burst while worshipping in the Catholic Church, because I thought that with a Baptist background, I knew it all.

I had recently joined the EE (Evangelism Explosion) Program in my church. It seemed as if God did not do enough harm to me by placing me on a team with one of the quietest, calmest, gentlest, stubbornest Catholic men I have ever met, the late Jim Lamb, but on top of that, one night he made our team get into a discussion about the Word of God. To my dismay this quiet, calm, gentle, stubborn Catholic man told me that the King James version of the Bible I had was rubbish, it was wrong, it was not the true Bible, etc.

Needless to say, I was fit to be tied. As I mentioned before, he was quiet, calm, etc. However, most of you who know me, know that I am the complete opposite: loud, bouncing, vibrant, etc. What a team. Sometimes you wonder if God worked this one out right. Or maybe, just maybe, you say to yourself, "God, really messed up this time!"

Well, I stormed back into the EE classroom. Everyone knew within minutes that I was upset. *I mean, my Bible? Wrong?* But wait a minute, there is only one Bible. Even if the translations were not worded the same, there was only one Bible. Yet my team leader was telling me my Bible was not correct? What did he know? I got my training from the Baptists. They know the Bible inside and out. He was a Catholic. What did he know?

For weeks I was raving mad. This madness led to my finding out what he meant. I soon learned that there was a Catholic Bible with more books than the Bibles the Protestants used. I decided to budget for a Catholic Bible. I did not have to spend the money, however, because soon thereafter, the late Irma from church was moving.

She gave me some cards, books, manuals, and other things which I gladly accepted. Among the books she gave me were two Bibles. I did not even open them. I just placed them on my bookshelf with the other Bibles I had. I kept spare Bibles to give away when someone needed a Bible. I used to get Bibles by the case for the prisoners at the

Stockade, hence if anyone gave me a Bible I would always accept it.

One night I was in bed. I was thinking about this Bible business again. All of a sudden I jumped up with the thought, *Wait a minute, suppose one of the Bibles Irma gave me had in it those extra books.* I got up went to the bookcase and opened them. Sure enough they were Catholic Bibles.

I looked through them and got the shock of my life. They had in them the other books of the Bible. Books such as Tobit, Judith, Sirach, Maccabees, Ecclesiasticus, Baruch. I was spellbound. I said, "What in Heaven's name is the meaning of this?" I was confused and angry at the same time. I wanted to know which was the correct Bible. Who printed these Bibles? Who changed them? Who took away? Who added? I was talking to God so loud I was shaking. Only thing is, when I talk to God the way I was talking to him, I never hear anything he has to say until I quiet down.

I decided to read the books. I read a story about a man who had a beautiful daughter. Every time she married a husband and they entered the bridal chamber they died. She was in one part of the world. She prayed to God to send her someone who would live. There was a man of God in another part of the world. He was also praying and asking God to send his son a wife.

One day this father had to send his son to the country where this girl was living. He met a man through his journeys who led him all the way. He met this girl; they fell in love and were married. The man whom the son had met told him what to do in order that he would not die in the bridal chamber. He heeded all the man told him. Soon he was taking his bride home to meet his father. At the end, the son turned to the man who helped him, to repay him for all he had done. The man told him he wanted nothing because he was an angel from God who was sent specifically to guard and lead him because God had heard the prayers of those praying.

That night I sat in bed and cried myself sick. I said, "Oh God, what a beautiful story. How could anyone have taken this out of the Bible and why?" No answer from God.

The very next day, my girlfriend who worked at another office on Brickell, and whom I had not seen for years, was telling me at lunch that she had recently bought a house and moved into it, but she said for some reason she could not sleep there. Her children had the same feeling. She said the night before she had been terribly afraid. Nothing like this had ever happened to her before. I told her I would pray for her that night.

As I was praying for her, in my prayers I said, "Lord, just as you sent an angel to minister to that couple in the Bible, please send an angel over to Beverly's house tonight to minister to them and give them sleep."

The next day during lunch, I forgot to ask Beverly what had happened last night. But just as we were finishing and going our separate ways, I said, "I almost forgot, did you sleep well last night?"

She shouted, "Elnieda, let me tell you what happened. I decided to light a candle because the house was so dark. I laid on my back and looked up, the glow of the candle made the image of Jesus on the wall."

I just smiled and said thank God.

Right there on the steps of the office I told her about the book in the Bible I had read and how I had asked God to send an angel. We joined hands, said a prayer and thanked God by saying, "Oh God, thank you for hearing our prayers, thank you that you did not even send an angel but you showed up. How great you are. Thank you that you not only heard prayers then, but you are still hearing and answering them today."

I went back to my office wondering how could anything so beautiful be taken from the Bible; who did it? This stayed with me for a long time. It truly bothered me.

By this time, I had started a Bible study in our office. I was a secretary in a large and prominent law firm. Some of the secretaries asked me, "Elnieda, why would you want to start a Bible study in a Jewish law firm?

I smiled and said, "That's precisely why."

The following Friday was the usual Bible study. The teacher started the class. During the class, he held up his Bible and said, "This is the Word of God, the true Word of God," I interrupted and said to him, "Tell me something, how can we go around waving our Bibles and saying this is the true Word of God when something is missing or added or taken out of them. Which is the true Word of God?"

This Bible teacher was once a Catholic. He had recently left the church. He started to tell me that there was some meeting in such and such year and it was decided at that meeting that the books taken from the Bible were not inspirational (or something to that effect). I said to him, "I don't want religion preached right now, I just want an explanation because the last page of this Bible I have in my hand says, 'Woe unto him who adds to this book, or who deletes from this book.'" We were going back and forth. To trigger this event, he said something about the Catholic Church being wrong. I said, "If we are Christians, it matters not what we think about each other, or what label we wear, so long as we preach and believe in Jesus Christ our Lord.

Therefore if you are going to cry down the church I worship in, or talk about any church being right or wrong, when they are all right and wrong, then I don't need your Bible study." I walked out. I really surprised myself because I had been to several Bible studies where I immediately realized that they were way off, but I would graciously excuse myself never more to return.

In this case however, immediately, immediately I stormed through that door, I got a headache. I mean a real whopper. I went back to my office. I sat at my desk shaking. Normally, when I had a headache I would place my hand on my head and pray. The headache would go away. This time, I placed my hand on my head, I prayed, the headache would not go away. I drank hot tea, the headache would not go away. About two hours later I felt so sick. I had to leave the office. I reached home and went to bed crying tears. The headache got worse. I got out of bed and went to my window. I pulled the drapes and started talking to God. I said, "Father, please, you are my only source now, please tell me what to do. I want so much to know you. How are we supposed to know if we don't even have the right book about you? Please talk to me, I need to know." Brothers and sisters, the Bible says, swear not; otherwise I would right now. But please take my word instead.

Immediately, I mean immediately, the Lord said to me, "That is not your business, you receive and accept what you have. You will not be held guilty for that. You have what you have, just believe. Those who have interfered with my Word will be the ones to answer to me. That is not your problem." My dear Brothers and sisters, I don't know what happens to you when the Lord talks to you but for me, at that time, my knees became weak. A flood of peace came over me from my head to the soles of my feet. This was not a hot healing feeling as I had experienced in the past. This was a brush of cool air like a gentle breeze. My windows were closed so I knew no air was coming into the apartment. As quickly as this happened, is as quickly as my headache completely left.

In the same breath, I sat down on the bed, picked up the telephone and called the Bible teacher. I said, "I would like to apologize for the manner in which I stormed out of the class today. However I would like you to know that I will not be coming back." He said to me, "Elnieda I accept your apology but what I said was facts." I said to him, "I did not call you to discuss factualities, I just wanted to apologize, please pray for me and I will pray for you." We hung up.

Thank God, from that day I have received such a peace over the Bible that I read them all, I enjoy them all, so I pass this on to anyone who questions the various variations of the Bible, hoping that this may help them. I would also ask that you read them for yourself. His Word changes not. God will answer us, only problem is, he answers us in his time.

Jim was right, people played havoc with the Bible but God will be the Judge of those who "takes out", not us. Praise his Holy name.

The Best Is Yet to Come

The Villages, FL 32163

I know that God is not only the author and finisher of my life, but he is also the author and finisher of this my book.

Why? Because after disobeying my mother, marrying to the wrong man, struggling so hard, starting life over and over again, going through life changes, life seasons, life storms, (including four surgeries, two major ones, twice I had to be hospitalized over 30 days, once learning to walk again), yet I have lived to experience victories and many countless blessings. I can therefore say, my brothers and sisters in Christ Jesus, Ladies and Gentlemen, *that* I have found favor with God, *that* now I truly await my harvest knowing *that* the *Best is yet to come!!!*

Since my born-again experience, I have always relied on God to provide *everything* for me. I do nothing before asking him. There were times when I thought I truly heard from him, so I ventured into what I thought he said, only to fall on my face. Whenever I fall, I do not lay there in self pity. *I get up, stand up and rise again.* With these falls I have come to truly understand the meaning of, "who can know the mind of God?" He is infinite all by himself.

There were times when I thought he was going to provide this for me through one source but his provision would come from an entirely different, unexpected source.

Blows your mind! What? Who would ever have thought? Only God knows!

Recently I heard a preacher say, "God will sabotage our plans to lead us in the right direction." Yep, he sure does! He will *make* you surrender, don't be afraid to do so, it will be a *sweet surrender.*

You will also come to know that he *makes* you confront and deal with all the junk and skeletons you have hidden in your closets. Especially those in your past. Yet you will find that he is so gentle, he does not allow them to tumble out all at once to harm you. You will find that he brings them out one at a time. Then, after you have repented and dealt with that one, you skip and dance and leap for joy feeling so clean and happy moving along and then… whoops! Out pops another. Each time you are given the grace and strength to deal with them until…all gone!

From then on, by the power of his Holy Spirit, you know without a shadow of a doubt when you are about to venture into another mess, so with fear and trembling you steer clear, remembering your past messes, literally being afraid to go back to a mess—you press on, avoiding it as hard as you can, to abide under the shelter of his wings, into his amazing saving grace.

Then and only then, my brothers and sisters, will you be able to boast about his Grace and Mercy and expound to others, "If he did it for me, he *will* do it for you." Praise his holy name forever and ever. Amen!

I know and believe that the *best is yet to come* because during these years of walking with the Lord, I have come to know that God will use you in ways you never imagined or dreamt of, if you completely surrender your all to him. There were times in my life, God would take me into places to be used by him that I would have to pause for a while, take stock of where I was, tears welling in my eyes, such wonderment in my mind I could only look up to him and say, *wow*.

For instance, my first time entering a prison to minister, my first time attending Bible classes, my first time going on a Christian Weekend Retreat, my first time leading a Life In The Spirit Group; My first time publicly speaking; my first time serving the Holy Eucharist. Those awesome times made me look back on my life. Way back!

Good

For most of us, life was good. Good because we were young and had happy times. Good because we had no care in the world. Good because we were healthy, we laughed, we loved, we played, we danced, we lived only one day at a time, without responsibilities.

Better

For most of use life was better. Better because we grew up; we married; we had children; we raised our children; sent them to better schools than we ever attended; we worked hard, we played hard, we planned life; we created bills, mortgages, cars, insurances, etc., you name it; our children grew up and took their places in society, whatever it might be. Yes, life was better.

We acquired and achieved. Then we downloaded, gave away, and simply stopped. So we retired, looked forward to a new changed lifestyle believing that *the best is yet to come.*

At retirement, some of us, like myself, in the 2005 era, lost all, or mostly all of what we had acquired, achieved, etc.

Upon my losing-it-all, in December 2007, my son, Wade, purchased a beautiful four bedroom house in Ocala, Central Florida, for me to live in. Not only did my son purchase this home for me, but he also gave me a new car.

I loved my new home. I enjoyed living in it. Yes, I was living in my better years, no small condo or townhouse. I had no idea that even *better* was around the corner until my sister retired and moved to The Villages, also located in Central Florida. I moved in with her, renting out the home in Ocala.

Why was it *better*? Because while living in Ocala I discovered The Villages. I loved it. I wanted to live there. Dreamt of living there. Visualized living there but, of course, we had already purchased in Ocala and could not sell as it was not a sellers' market.

Neither my sister nor I ever dreamt that one day we would be living together in Florida. To me, living in The Villages is *better* than living in Ocala, at least where we had bought.

The Best Is Yet to Come

Most of us have always taken the words: *good, better, best* for granted. But as we grew older and we have been there, done that, we find ourselves also reflecting on the *good, the bad, and the ugly* in our past. We come to the place in our lives that we often change our perspective of life and what lies ahead of us. We think not only of the *bad* and *ugly* things we did, but of the *good* things we did/achieved, the *better* things we accomplished. Now we aim/look forward to the *best* to come.

We have come to realize that life sometimes consists of so many highs and lows, ups and downs, hills and valleys, fall downs, get ups and rises, beginnings and endings—that sooner or later we MUST insist, talk to ourselves and believe that *the best is yet to come, this ain't it!*

As of today, July 28, 2013, I am definitely living in my better years, with the corporate world of stress behind me, three grown children, two grown grandsons, concentrating on myself, dancing with singles groups, enjoying old and new friends, blessed by God with good health and, most of all, walking and talking with him daily.

I thank him for so many things, for the fact that I look so good at the age of seventy-three, for my hair which I lost from stress growing back, for the acne scars cleaning up off my face, I still have my silky skin, my features, most of all that I am his child and he takes care and provide for my every need.

Our Heavenly Father deserves to be thanked, praised, adored, and worshipped daily.

At the time of writing this book, my one prayer is yet to be answered—*my Boaz to come into my life.* My friends have always told me, "Elnieda, you have been praying over twenty-five years for him and he has not come. Give up, God wants you for himself." I always reply, "No! if that is so, he would take away those desires from my body. Desires that intensify year after year. Furthermore, God made man for woman and woman for man. Only God knows!"

So, year after year I continue to pray—pray it up Elnieda, dream on Elnieda, dream on because your *best is yet to come!!* And so I wait…

Despite Our Mess and Ignorance

The Villages, Florida 32163

Friends of the Good Shepherd

For almost one year, I felt that the Lord wanted me to do more for him. I felt I was being led to work with the poor. I knew it was not the poor in Miami because I knew many churches were in fact deeply committed to working with them already. They all did excellent jobs. Eventually, after much praying, I realized that the poor I was to work with were in Jamaica. I thought I was to move back to Jamaica. This idea of moving back to Jamaica stayed with me for so long, until finally one day my son and I discussed the possibilities of my moving back. We decided that I should just go.

I took this conversation with my son, and this final decision, as confirmation from the Lord, that I should go.

I gave up my apartment in Dadeland, leaving Sister Beatrice, a nun who was living with me, there. Sent most of my furnishings to my son's condo in Kendall and I left for Jamaica, October 1, 1992.

On the fifth of October, I headed for Port Antonio to find a place to live as I had already decided that I did not want to live in Kingston. I needed peace and quiet. I wanted a villa to house my friends whenever they visited me in Jamaica. I found a place on the hills overlooking Frenchman's Cove, in San San, Port Antonio.

On my return to Kingston, after working out the figures and monthly payments, I said to the Lord, "Lord, the house I just saw is such a luxury place. Also, the house I am staying in, on Beverly Hills is also a luxury place, I feel out of touch with the poor. If I am coming here to work for and with the poor shouldn't I be with the poor?" This thought lingered with me so much that I had to seek a Word from the Lord. I opened the Bible at random and landed on James 2. James was speaking about the rich and the poor. I said, "Lord, are you trying to tell me that it is okay to live in luxury as the rich also need you? Are you trying to tell me to minister to the rich?"

At this time, the domestic helper for the home in which I was staying came to work. We started to chit chat. Our conversation quickly came around to the Lord. She was so full of his Holy Spirit she was actually rich. Rich in spirit, but at that time I could not see it because I was not looking for that. All I knew was, something was wrong with this picture. I was supposed to be working with the poor, ministering to them, yet here she was, a poor helper, ministering to and with me. Her faith was so strong.

I was frustrated. I decided I needed the Body, I needed help. I got the telephone book and found a Catholic Charismatic number. I called them and after speaking for a while with one Rena, she gave me Father HoLung's telephone number. I called Father HoLung's office. He was not in. I spoke with an Indian priest who had answered the phone. We talked for a long time. He wanted to know why I did not stay in Miami and help from there as I would be more effective being in Miami. I told him no, because I also wanted to sort of semi-retire, live in Port Antonio, and be among the poor. I told him that I did not want to help Father HoLung because I knew June was already helping him, neither did I want to help Father Albert, because I knew Coleen was helping him. I wanted to find a priest in a poor area somewhere in the country hills to work with.

I was beginning to get frustrated with him because I did not like the idea of him mentioning I should stay in Miami, when I knew that the Lord had sent me to Jamaica, the prime reason why I was here.

He then said "You know, I think you need to talk with the Chancery." He gave me the number, we hung up. This was about 11:00 a.m. on Wednesday the seventh of October.

I went to lie down. My mind was tired. I did not want to talk to anyone else. At about 3:00 p.m. I decided to call the Chancery. I did. I talked with the lady on the phone for a while, explaining what I needed, she said, "I think you had better talk with the archbishop."

The archbishop, Archbishop McCarter, came on the telephone and I explained to him that I needed a poor parish in the country to work with as I felt that the Lord was leading me to work with the poor in Jamaica. He said, "When you say poor, what do you mean?" Immediately

James 2 became vividly clear and real to me, *Poor in spirit.* I did not answer. He said, "You know, sometimes the rich is poor and the poor is rich." I said "Yes, I know"—remembering the conversation I had with the helper. He kept talking, I could say nothing because I knew that the Lord was talking through him. He said, "I really believe you should help in Kingston, because most people in the country areas move into Kingston trying to make it and instead they end up being here. Leaving us with twice the number of people to take care of. I am going to give you the names and numbers of three priests in Kingston whom you may be able to help." He gave them to me.

After I hung up, I said, "Lord, you know I don't want to be in Kingston, I want to be in Port Antonio, but your will be done."

The next morning I called the first number. No answer. I called the second number, Father Kenneth Ramsay answered. I told him that Archbishop McCarter had given me his number and what I wanted to do. He said "I don't believe it."

I said "What don't you believe, father?"

He said, "Just two days ago I told the archbishop, "I cannot do it. This church you had sent me to build has nothing. I have to start from scratch with nothing. How are we going to do it?" But the archbishop just said to me, "Don't worry, God will provide."

I am thinking, *Provide? Provide through someone like me? This is crazy, but Praise you, Jesus!*

Brothers and sisters, needless to say, that blew my mind and I started to cry. I don't know if you got the depth of this but because I knew me, because I knew where I was coming from, the depth and realization of this calling suddenly came over me and now that it was truly happening, I could not believe that God would really use someone like me to "provide" for his work!

I said, "Oh, father, praise the Lord, I knew God brought me here, but I just did not know how it would turn out. I guess I was going into the wrong areas. Nothing came together until I called the Body." Father Ramsay said he would pick me up the next morning and take me over to where he was stationed.

The following morning, Saturday the tenth of October, Father Ramsay picked me up and we headed for Portmore. I thought, *Portmore? Oh, Lord, no, Portmore? It was in that same area, where I met a male friend in a hotel, near that same church, near my home. Oh, Lord, no. Not Portmore?*

Independence City is beside Portmore. I had purchased my first house over twenty years before in Independence City. I don't want to go back to that area.

I kept quiet while Father Ramsay gave me a tour. The area was four times the size it used to be; it had grown so much I was amazed. Finally, Father Ramsay took me to see some model units being built.

I went into one, looked around and immediately began analyzing how to enlarge the kitchen, expand the living area, widen the bedroom, etc. Then all of a sudden, like a big bang, I said to myself, "Elnieda, are you crazy, what are you doing, the first house you bought over twenty years ago was twice the size of this, at your age what are you talking about building this and adding that?" I got so cold with fear I ran out of the house and stood by the car. I was literally shaking. I was so disturbed. How could this be?

God called me to Jamaica. I went. I was with a priest who needed help, and now I wanted to chicken out. I didn't want to be there. What was going on? I just stood by the car saying to myself, over and over again, "I can't do it. I can't do it."

While I was standing there, Father Ramsay came out of the other house walking as fast as he could. He came straight towards me saying "You know Elnieda, I don't think you should really come here to live and start building and building again." I almost passed out. I said, "What did you say, father?."

He repeated himself and said, "We really don't need another pair of extra hands. The poor here love the Lord and they serve the Lord. I can always get hands to work. What we need is help. The people are always looking to God for help. They believe with all their hearts that God will send them help. If you come here to be with them, sooner or later, you will be just like them. You will start acting like them, talking like them, and being like them. I know you want to evangelize and all that, but you know the people come to Father HoLung. He really does not go out looking for them per se. People will always come to us when they need help, and help is what they need." I said "Father, I don't believe you said that, I just came out here thinking the same thing. I just don't believe it." We left the site and I took him to have dinner. By this time, I was thinking, *What now?* But I said, "Lord, your will be done. I give up."

At dinner, Father Ramsay looked at me and said, "You know, Elnieda, I really believe you should stay in Miami and help us."

I replied, "Father, you really believe that, but I know the Lord wanted me to come to Jamaica."

He said, "Yes, I know, but I really believe you would be more effective for us being there. And maybe this is the Lord speaking. Think about it, because I could see you helping us much more being over there. I don't want to paint a doom and gloom picture to you, but you would be much better off over there in Miami." I said "Father, why is everyone telling me to stay in Miami, when you all are here?", He said, "Because we have taken a vow and we go wherever we are sent."

I got the message, loud and clear.

Father took me to the church site for The Church of the Good Shepherd located in Portmore, St Catherine, Jamaica, West Indies. Father Kenneth Ramsay is the pastor. It is a small wooden church being built mostly by American volunteers (see the photos included in this book). It was originally intended to be a clinic but because there was no church in the area to use for services it is being used as both a clinic and a church. The government of Jamaica donated the land to build the main church, a school and the pastor's residence.

Father said, "This is where you will come in, Elnieda, to help us from Miami. Right now I need everything, stationary, envelopes, business cards, supplies, etc., to introduce us into the area."

I listened intently. These were things that I could readily supply because I had this kind of shop in Miami, which father knew nothing about. All these things I could prepare myself through Trinity Copying Services, Inc. I smiled; God knew this, so He arranged the entire trip/meeting. I told father about my shop and told him it was done.

After giving father some money for gas and a few dollars to start a bank account for the church, I left Jamaica with a very excited feeling.

How I thought my mission was going to happen, it did not happen. It did happen, however, but in His way. All I knew was, I had a mission, and that I had to go to Jamaica to discover what that mission was. Thank God.

Brothers and sisters, after my visit to Jamaica, the meaning of James 2 became very vivid to me, in that, if we are not able to travel over the world to preach the Word of God, we can just be planted where we are, *being* the Word of God, thus by our giving and caring, people will come to know Jesus our Savior through us. That's evangelization. James 2 says, "If your brother comes to you hungry, will you tap him on the shoulders and say, 'the Lord be with you' and send him away hungry? What good will that be? Show me your works and I will show you your faith." Amen.

I returned to Miami on October 15, 1992, and formed a 501c not-for-profit corporation in Miami, Florida, in the name of The Friends of the Good Shepherd. The first thing I did with this corporation was to seek help from family and friends as per the following letter.

THE FRIENDS OF THE GOOD SHEPHERD
844 Brickell Plaza, Miami, FL 33131

Sometime ago I wrote to you letting you know that I was going to Jamaica to take up residency because I felt the Lord was leading me to work with the poor. I went to Jamaica on October 1, 1992. I cannot go into the [details] of my visit in this letter, but after talking with the late Archbishop Carter, two priests, and others; it was very evident that I would better serve the needs of the poor in Jamaica if I stayed here in Miami. So I returned to Miami and hence the formation of "The Friends of the Good Shepherd."

I will be, with the help of friends such as yourself, supporting, assisting, building a Church in Jamaica, named "The Church of the Good Shepherd," pastored by Rev. Father Kenneth Ramsay.

The purpose of this letter therefore is to ask if you would be generous enough to give us a dollar per week toward this seed planting effort. Please believe me when I say a dollar per week will be enough, because one US dollar is equivalent to twenty-two dollars in Jamaica and your dollar will go a far way.

I know that America, and indeed the entire world is going through very hard economic times but when you see the hurting people in Jamaica, especially the children you will understand why I have decided to beg for them. As a Christian, Jamaican, American, I believe with all my heart that one of the main reasons why America is so blessed is because she gives to the world. Even to her enemies. America has given in abundance. Jesus tells us, "I am the Bread of Life" and that we should feed His sheep. I am reaching out to you and ask that you become his friend to the poor in Jamaica by sending me one dollar per week or four dollars per month. Your gift is tax deductible.

Please feel free to call me if you need more information on either The Church of the Good Shepherd or The Friends of The Good Shepherd. God richly bless you in your giving.

In his name
Elnieda Telfer Sinclair
President

Summary

This book is about the journey of a twenty-three year old divorced Jamaican woman, with three babies, ranging from one to three years old, who was determined to provide a home and obtain the best life she possibly could for herself and her children. In her twenties, she migrated to the United States of America, where she lived and worked in New York City.

Three years later, she returned to her native country, Jamaica. Most of her life she worked two jobs to survive. They lived a modest life. As the years went by, they had a good life. In their late teens, the children left Jamaica for a better life in America with family members.

Tired and exhausted, in 1978, Elnieda once again emigrated to the United States, this time taking up residence in Miami, Florida.

After three months, depressed and feeling sorry for herself, one Saturday morning she began yelling and cursing at God, blaming him for everything negative that had happened to her, only to encounter a head-on collision with our Lord Jesus Christ. She was knocked out for hours on the floor. When she came to, she realized that there was a God, that he was real and alive. She thought to herself, *God is not to be messed with.*

From that day her life took a hundred-eighty-degree drastic change, from her world to His world.

Afterword

Some who read this may say, "This is her life, so what? Who cares?" But I, a young woman, struggling from the age of eighteen—worked it. Achieved it. Lost it. Started over and over again, only to have it, then lose it again. Yet *never* gave up. *Never* allowed myself to have a pity party but each time *got up, stood up, and rose* above it.

With all my heart—I feel that somewhere, someplace, somehow, there is someone who will benefit from my life's story, and they too will "get up, stand up, and rise," believing that "If God could allow Elnieda to do it, then so can I! Because he will do the same for me."

Even though I had no personal relationship with my Lord and Savior Jesus Christ in the beginning, I know now that he was always with me, whether or not I knew it. He gave me a second chance in life to repent and turn my life around. Then he gave me third, fourth, fifth, and endless chances. He will do the same for you. Please know that he is also with you and he will turn your life around, if you but ask him. Ask him! He is waiting, earnestly and tenderly calling your name.

Thank God for his infinite mercies, and as the old folks in Jamaica used to say, "Thank God for Jesus." I never knew the full meaning of those words, but now I do.

And so I Get Up...

Stand Up...

and Rise...

About the Author

Elnieda was born on the Island of Jamaica in the West Indies. In her early twenties she emigrated to the United States of America, taking up residence in New York. After three years, she returned to Jamaica.

Because of the political upheaval in Jamaica, Elnieda returned to America in August 1978, landing at Miami International Airport with twelve dollars. She resided in Miami, Florida, where she worked as a secretary.

In February 1979, Elnieda had a tremendous conversion experience, which changed her life drastically, drawing her towards a personal relationship with the Lord Jesus Christ. Through this conversion, she was led to a Baptist church where she became grounded in the Word for two years. As a child, Elnieda was raised in both the Catholic and the Methodist churches. However, her heart and roots were in the Catholic Church.

Between 1979 to 1981, while working as a secretary, she volunteered at the Veterans Hospital on Saturdays and The Dade County Stockade on Sundays. During her lunch hour, she volunteered at Camillus House.

In 1981, while studying the Word, the Word led her back to the Catholic Church, where she grew in leaps and bounds.

Then in 1984, she received her certificate as a trainer in Evangelism Explosion III International.

By 1985, she was awarded a certificate as a lay teacher/trainer in Evangelism Explosion III International.

Between 1984 to 1986, while in the Catholic Church, she volunteered at the Miami Dade Correctional Center—taking prisoners to church on Sundays.

In 1990, both her hands collapsed from carpal tunnel syndrome, and she was no longer able to type as a secretary. The Lord then gave her a business, which she named after Him, Trinity Copying Services, Inc., later changed to Trinity Graphics & Copy Center, Inc.

Then in 1992, she founded a not-for-profit corporation, The Friends of the Good Shepherd, to assist in the building of the Church of the Good Shepherd located in Jamaica.

In 1995, in order to save her business, Elnieda rented out her condo fully-furnished, and moved into her shop, sleeping on the floor at times, to make her shop work.

By June 7, 2002, she expanded The Friends of the Good Shepherd into a foundation.

The two hurricanes in 2005, Katrina and Wilma, devastated the area where her shop was located in Miami causing a slowdown in business. This was a setback. She lost money and business. She sought the help of a young partner to take over the shop.

Finally in December 2007, she retired and moved to Ocala, in Central Florida, into a house purchased for her by her son.

Religious Activities

From 1981-1995, Elnieda was a very active member of St. Louis Catholic Church while she lived in Southwest Miami.

In years 1995-2007, Elnieda moved from the Southwest to Downtown Miami to be closer to her shop. She then became a member of St. Jude Melkite Catholic Church, where she sang in the choir and was secretary to The Ladies Guild.

In July 2008, Elnieda became a member of Immaculate Heart of Mary Catholic Church in Ocala, Central Florida, where she became active as a Eucharist minister, a sacristan, and a facilitator of the Why Catholic home group.

Then in January 2013, Elnieda moved to The Villages, in Central Florida. In March of the same year, she became a member of St. Vincent de Paul Catholic Church. She is presently a Eucharistic minister and a member of the Small Christian Community (SCC) Group at St. Vincent de Paul.

Ministries and businesses Elnieda was involved in before her retirement:

1. Eucharistic minister/sacristan
2. Team leader, Evangelization Explosion
3. Team leader, Life in the Spirit Seminars
4. President, Trinity Graphics & Copy Center, Inc.
5. President, Friends of the Good Shepherd
6. Volunteer, Veterans Hospital for 6 years
7. Volunteer, Miami Correctional Institution for 3 years
8. Member, Black Business Association
9. Member, Chamber of Commerce
10. Member, Brickell Area Association

Elnieda believes her greatest achievement was raising her three children as a single parent.

On Thursday, July 26, 2012, through a revelation given to me on this day by an author, Matthew Kelly, while reading his book *The Rhythm of Life* in a church home group—at age seventy-two—I was inspired to start writing this book.